MW01169843

# Starting Over

# Praise for *Starting Over*

"Everyone has had a life-changing experience either forced upon them or by their own choice. It's easy to fall into depression, anger and to become paralyzed into inaction when change happens. Will does an excellent job of explaining the root of these emotions, how they manifest themselves, how to navigate through them and, most importantly, how to keep moving forward."

**Eugene Hashimoto,** mergers and acquisitions strategist

"This book will make a great companion for anyone who is going through one of life's big transitions."

**Michael J. Maloney,** President, Global OEM, D&M Holdings

"The ideas in this book were an anchor during the difficult times in my career journey. The path you choose makes all the difference."

**Todd Sheppelman,** CEO, Air International Thermal Systems

"Know thyself! This is a fundamental tenet for any new venture in life, whether it's the hunt for a new job, starting a new role, getting past the trauma of sickness or facing any life challenge. The principle is to prepare before moving on to something new.

Will's book drew me to introspection about the success and happiness I sought and eventually found. More importantly, Will's compelling words drove me to focus on the future and not get mired in the past. Getting prepared, getting the impetus to look forward, and focus are my keys to finding happiness in career and life. I will refer to this book many times as the excitement of life unfolds."

**Christine Filipowicz,** Vice President, Plasan NA

# Starting Over

## Renewing Life in Transition

*To my friend Tony —*
*For all of the times you have*
*started over, and will again —*
*Will Ellis*

### WILL ELLIS, PhD

iUniverse, Inc.
New York  Bloomington

**Starting Over**
**Renewing Life in Transition**

Photo Credits: Cover photo *A New Day* taken by Will Ellis

The photos of the Great Wallendas and Alex Wallenda from the
Wallenda Family Archives used with permission of Tino Wallenda

iUniverse books may be ordered through booksellers or by contacting:

iUniverse
1663 Liberty Drive
Bloomington, IN 47403
www.iuniverse.com
1-800-Authors (1-800-288-4677)

ISBN: 978-1-4401-9029-2 (sc)
ISBN: 978-1-4401-9031-5 (dj)
ISBN: 978-1-4401-9030-8 (ebk)

Printed in the United States of America

iUniverse rev. date: 11/11/2009

*To Rob, Kristin, Bill, and Adam*
*for teaching me more than I could ever teach you.*

# Contents

# Preface

10,000 miles, fare thee well
My own true love, farewell for a while
I'm going away, but I'll be back
Though I go 10,000 miles[1]

"10,000 Miles," a beautiful song by Mary Chapin Carpenter, tells the story of a long journey and the pain of separation and loss. It strikes a universal chord with any of us who have lived a bit of this life, because anyone who has lived has lost.

If someone were walking, a journey of ten thousand miles would seem like such a long distance. We might be willing to walk ten thousand miles to get a past life back, if only we could. But life moves ahead and time always moves forward, so we don't have that option.

If a journey of one thousand miles starts with a single step, how does a journey of ten thousand miles start? The same way, one foot in front of the other. The first step in any journey is the hardest. If we just take it, we can get there.

We experience misfortune and loss in our lives in thousands of ways, and no matter how well we understand that fact in our heads, our hearts still break. When we lose someone we love from a terminal illness, even if we know months ahead, the finality is still difficult to accept. It is at tender times like these that we reach out for a hand to hold to soften the pain, to gain steadiness, to make sense of it all.

We leave deep fingernail tracks in the door frames of life—a testament to our struggle to cling to what we know, hoping to stay where we are. Life, nonetheless, boots us through to the other side. Even when we plead for life to leave us alone, when it seems as if we've learned enough lessons for an entire lifetime, waves of change continue to rise.

The experience of reinventing oneself brings to mind one of my favorite quotes attributed to Mother Teresa: "I know God will not give me anything I can't handle. I just wish He didn't trust me so much." Life renewal can be really hard.

And yet, starting over is simply the dance of creation as we fulfill an embedded purpose—to grow. It's the blessing of being alive and clearly better than the alternative. This book is intended as a guide for anyone with a chapter that is ending, whether or not the next chapter has been written. It is meant to help navigate through the emotional as well as the rational ebbs and flows of the white water of change.

People who are successful in transformation frame change in a way that builds capacity, including the emotional intelligence, to accept the challenge.

*Starting Over* is a reflection on the journey of people in transition. It is a reminder of something we all know, at some level, about the pain in loss and letting go, but it is also about the joy in discovering something better ahead.

This book speaks to the value in understanding the cycles and patterns that life brings. The many personal stories and examples here are included for a reason. This is not only a book about work and careers, but about life.

From yet another view, this is really a story about the power of compassion, of support for one another, and ultimately of love in helping each other through life.

If you believe like I do that we are all here on earth to learn lessons from others and in turn to offer our own lessons, this is the message that I am here to share. I hope this book helps you to connect to the patterns in your life and lifts you through to the next step in your journey.

# Introduction

After more than thirty years of coaching organizations and their leaders, I want to share a message of hope, even in the darkest times. The Great Recession that picked up steam in 2008 brought unprecedented change. Driven by a perfect storm of interdependent forces, the recession touched everyone at some level.

A hailstorm of economic pain was unleashed in a frenzied downward spiral of organizational restructuring, intense fear of job loss, actual job loss, the bursting of the housing bubble, and then mortgage defaults. The unbelievable crumbling of some of our most revered financial institutions fed the cycle, triggering a generalized collapse in spending and even further job loss.

*Fired. Laid off. Furloughed. Forced retirement. Downsized. Outplaced.* This collection of words has become commonplace in our vocabulary. Well-orchestrated downsizing by our nation's employers has become almost an art form, with roots that go back decades and processes perfected in recent times. It seems as if any manager with experience has gone through this rite of passage. For some, "letting people go" has become a well-honed skill.

Companies used to struggle to keep people employed in tough times. Loyalty to employees, who responded with loyalty to the organization in return, has become a lost value in our culture.

Stockholder pressure to perform and the increased presence of highly leveraged private equity investors have reduced our tolerance for financial loss. Right or wrong, financial pressure is a reality. As a result, many of us have lives that look a lot different than they did five or ten years ago. The game is changing fast.

At some point in our lives, each of us is faced with the challenge of starting over. We leave a comfort zone where we are strong and comfortable, an existence we know, and life invites us to begin again. From the womb to the world, from home to school, from school to work, from job to job, from work to retirement, on and on, our lives take us on a journey of change. We jump, voluntarily or not, into our next life phase and—hopefully—renewal.

The mission of this book is to assist anyone who experiences a fundamental change in his or her work life—for any person who has hit a wall. For people trying to survive the rapidly changing world of work, that might mean being laid off, retired by choice or force, or maybe even fired. The economy has brought unprecedented change to most of us. These times are a reminder that our work lives are fragile.

Is it true that experiences that don't kill us make us stronger? The difficult passages in life are the occasions that develop our character and define us. They are the formative events in which we grow the most, despite the fact that we may never ask for those changes.

If you are about to leave or have already left one stage of your life and are thinking about the next, there may be something here for you.

This writing is also for people who have purposely chosen to move on from a past that no longer works, with hope for something better. We always imagine leaving a bad work relationship or retiring as an extremely positive event, but the same challenges apply in getting through the transition.

Many people say that retirement is the most difficult life transition they have experienced. Underneath the sleeping-in, extra vacation trips, and just hanging out is the challenge of a major life shift. Step change is always hard.

## Starting Over

Whatever the situation you find yourself in, you are moving on to the next phase in your work and your life. There is no going back, and the task of making the best of this life is still before you. You are ready to move ahead.

This story is about being let go and about letting go. Let's get started.

# 1

## A New Economic Reality

> "Vitality shows in not only the ability to
> persist but the ability to start over."
>
> —F. Scott Fitzgerald

### A Fragile World

On August 21, 1985, AT&T dropped a bombshell on the world when the company announced it would be laying off twenty-four thousand Information Systems employees, a headcount reduction in the company not seen since 1933 during the Great Depression. While rumors of the change had circulated for months, the finality of it all was a shock to everyone.

I was leading a workshop with a group from the Information Systems Division that day. Word of the layoffs spread quickly through the meeting, despite the fact that this was long before mobile phones, instant messages, and e-mail. Human beings find ways to communicate when they want to.

The looks on the faces of the affected employees is something that I will never forget. As the story emerged, my meeting participants were devastated. They were full of shock, denial, anger, indignation, and bewilderment.

"No way! How could this happen to us? How could it happen to me? I am not going to stand for this! Why me?"

Suddenly my sermon about being a good team leader seemed much less relevant to the people in that room. Twenty-four thousand people had just hit a wall in their lives, and the grief cycle had begun.

The headlines in *USA Today* were brief and factual, but between the lines of print there were twenty-four-thousand personal stories to tell, and they were all complex, each with the thousands of details that a life can simultaneously hold.

Many had expected another shoe to drop after the federally mandated breakup of AT&T the year before. The company had been broken into the regional Bell Companies plus two divisions of the mother company, but mass employee layoffs were still a relatively new thing to the world, much less at AT&T. They had been a monopoly for so many years—the epitome of a safe-haven employer. If one were loyal and didn't break the law, working at AT&T could mean a job for life, or so everyone thought.

The original AT&T is a great example of an organization that became so ensconced in its pattern for success that, eventually, this pattern triggered its very demise. The company started out as the Bell Telephone Company in 1877, founded by Alexander Graham Bell and several financial investors, just one year after Bell had introduced his version of the telephone. In 1885, Bell Telephone was renamed the American Telephone & Telegraph Company (AT&T), establishing the first national telephone network in the United States.

In 1906, just over a hundred years ago, only 8 percent of households in the U.S. had a phone. In 1913, AT&T's President Theodore Vail helped to forge a deal with the federal government to anoint AT&T as a sanctioned monopoly. In exchange for high long distance rates and a regulated monopoly over the entire United States, AT&T committed to provide universal service—telephone access to every home, farm, and business in the country.

AT&T had to accept governmental oversight and allow independents access to their long distance lines, but why not? In many respects, AT&T was *the* phone company, the only game in town. Safe from competitors, the foundation of their future had been built.

It didn't really matter if any one portion of the company was profitable or not. Revenue from long distance service subsidized local calls. Money from calls in densely populated urban areas helped pay for rural calls at a time when a large portion of America consisted of farms spread far apart. Higher margin business systems supported the lower fees paid by residences.

If someone wanted phone service, he or she had to call (or visit) the phone company, AT&T. If an individual consumer wanted a phone to use on the network, he or she had to buy or lease one from AT&T. In 1927, a three-minute call from New York to London cost $75! There were no low-cost alternatives.

AT&T grew quickly during the 1920s. The Graham Act of 1921 kept AT&T exempt from the Sherman Antitrust Act, so the company was assured not only of survival, but of a "fair" profit as well.

For decades, AT&T stock was the most widely held in the world. Their employees achieved technological breakthroughs that helped the U.S. economy grow and the country thrive. The Bell Labs, the technical development arm of the company, produced eleven Nobel Prize winners. They developed the transistor in 1947, which the Justice Department required AT&T to license for $25,000. AT&T developed early versions of wireless phones, which they were not allowed to test in the marketplace until 1977. They also developed cell phones in the 1980s and Wi-Fi in the 1990s.

Despite all of these technological advances, the company never had to fight for market share in a free economy. When it was finally time to come out and compete again, the knowledge and the instinct were not there. It had been bred out. Cracks in AT&T's formula for success began to appear. In the 1960s, the Federal Communications

Commission began allowing independent companies to connect their equipment to AT&T's. By the 1970s consumers were allowed to purchase telephones from competitors and use them with AT&T service. AT&T may not have realized it yet, but they had hit their wall. The marketplace had shifted. Continued success for the company necessitated a new game plan—one that never came.

AT&T had created a monopoly that in their minds allowed a reprieve from worry about competition. Over time the company's cultural DNA didn't encourage looking outside the company or listening to their customers. It didn't matter what anyone else was doing.

When it was finally time to come out and compete again in a new market, the knowledge and the instinct were not there. It had been bred out of the organization.

At its apex, AT&T employed over a million people and earned more than $69 billion in annual revenue, a full 2 percent of the gross national product of the United States. Once change had begun, the course of the company's demise was set. AT&T was finally purchased on January 31, 2005, by SBC, a collection of some of the "Baby Bells," the local phone companies they had spawned back in 1984. By that time the workforce had been reduced to forty-seven thousand six hundred, with sales of just over $29 billion.

AT&T used large-scale layoffs to cut costs before doing so became the corporate fad *du jour*. Back in 1985, who could have predicted what was coming?

Futurists of the day began reciting a common chant about change occurring at a quicker pace, the impact of technology on the speed of everything, and life simply moving faster. Many of us at that time shared at least a little in the AT&T employees' belief, and maybe in their arrogance, that these massive changes wouldn't directly affect us. In the intervening years, however, a lot of people hit their walls too, as the world fundamentally changed.

## Lessons Learned

So what are the lessons from AT&T's story? First, AT&T was an organization full of very smart people who performed at high levels and who subsequently went on to other companies to perform well. They were good people caught up in a larger wave—an organizational force that had been defined years earlier. By committing and sticking to an immutable formula for success, the company also defined what it was *not*: it was not a tough competitor in a rapidly changing telecommunications industry.

Second, adaptation to change is critical for survival in a rapidly transitioning environment, no matter how good any of us *used to be*. If a radical shift could happen to AT&T, it can happen to any organization or to any person.

Third, radical changes happen to organizations that are very good at what they do. Every company and every living system that comes into being eventually dies. The principle of transiency, that in time everything changes, is an enduring rule of life.

No matter how smart we are, the formula for success that got us to where we are will not get us to the future. To survive, organizations and people need to change what they do.

Maybe the most important lessons lie in the experiences of the twenty-four thousand people who were let go by AT&T on that fateful day in 1985. Those AT&T employees may have been early pioneers in the downsizing experience, at least in the late twentieth century, but they certainly weren't the last. When we read about a large corporation laying off thousands of people today, we shrug our shoulders, numbed to the experience, a story so often told these days.

- *Kodak will cut up to 4,500 jobs.* "Sure, that's not surprising given the industry ... We could all see it coming."

- *General Motors targets 30,000 hourly jobs.* "Yes, didn't they do that already? Is this another layoff? Is this the old GM or the new GM?"

- *IBM may reduce headcount by 100,000, a third of their global workforce.* "Do they have that many people left? I thought they had already cut way back."

The economic recession that technically began in 2007 has set some new standards in our lifetime. The jobless rate reflects the biggest jump since the Great Depression and the duration of unemployment is the highest on record.[2]

Like it or not, we have entered into a new global economic reality. Organizations are facing real life-or-death challenges, forced to cut costs or cease to exist. Unprecedented global competition forces corporations to become more efficient, and one obvious way to do that is to reduce labor costs, or headcount. No one controls this trend; it is one of those many things in life that *just is.*

Whether fair or not, an extraordinary number of people are losing their jobs. Many take jobs that they are overqualified for just to make ends meet. Early retirements, buyouts, layoffs, reductions in workforce, voluntary or involuntary separations—no matter the tactic, the outcome is the same: a lot of people with lots of life energy are trying to cope with employment loss.

It's easy from a distance to become desensitized, but thousands of people are being dramatically affected. Every outplaced person represents a human life and a family whose lives are profoundly affected. These are real people, just like you and me. It is likely that at some point in our careers, they *are* you and me.

Nobody knows the endings to all of those twenty-four thousand stories from AT&T, but many probably did not end with the words *happily ever after.* The emotional and financial stress of losing one's job hurts.

On the other hand, in my coaching work, I have found that the most common story is in fact a positive one, despite the very difficult transition people face when they are outplaced. People move on with their lives. There is life after AT&T and after every other organization. Good people find work and often wonder why they didn't move sooner, of their own volition. Often the hardest part of the saga is waiting for the shoe to drop—dreading the anticipation of being let go as much as being let go.

I hope the majority of the twenty-four-thousand stories had good endings. There were, no doubt, surprises along with way, with some very difficult bumps along the road. Life rarely turns out the way we plan, but life has a way of working out. In the end, we usually get what we really need. If we are fortunate, we eventually see the purpose of these events and how they take our lives in directions we never would have guessed and from the broader perspective of life make all the difference.

Faith is an important element in getting through these unexpected transitions in life. No matter how bleak things seem at any moment, it is really important to trust that life does work out.

"This moment is the perfect teacher, and, lucky
for us, it's with us wherever we are."

—Pema Chödrön

# 2

## Hitting the Wall:
## The Unplanned Crises in Our Lives

"For everything there is a season, and a time
for every matter under heaven."

—Ecclesiastes 3:1

### A Significant Emotional Event

These days, many people find themselves in a place where they need to start over, experiencing a major shift of one form or another. Job loss, retirement, illness, loss of a loved one—the list of reasons is long. Some of these changes are anticipated and planned for; others are completely unexpected. But the result is the same: a familiar part of life ends and the next phase of the journey begins.

Eugene O'Kelly tells a gripping story of how, at age fifty-three and at the peak of his career and his life, he was diagnosed with late-stage brain cancer. In his book, *Chasing Daylight: How My Forthcoming Death Transformed My Life,* O'Kelly explains that he saw a blessing in his diagnosis.[3] Being told he had three months to live gave him an opportunity that many miss—to tell his friends and family what they had meant to him and to decide, while his thoughts were still lucid, how to spend the rest of his life.

Urgently scheduled MRIs revealed a complex and incurable web of cancer in the left hemisphere of his brain. These first meetings with his doctors brought on the classic reactions in O'Kelly: disorientation, surprise, and then shock as the weight of it all sank in. Suddenly thrust into the end stages of his life, this was it. Everything about his life had suddenly changed.

Ultimately we all die, but many don't have an opportunity to reflect on our lives at the end. Many are physically ill and cognitively incapacitated by their last days, and some pass quickly in an accident or by heart attack, without time to be thankful or to reflect without pain. O'Kelly saw the gift in having some time at the end when he was still feeling healthy, and he took advantage of every moment.

Eugene O'Kelly gave us some amazing gifts through his writings: We can be thankful for what we have right now. Whether our last days come ninety days or ninety years from now, we can consider what is truly important to accomplish on this earth and set about doing it. Unplanned crises happen to everyone, and we can always choose how we respond to them.

Many of the significant emotional events in our lives surprise us. We might know in our hearts that there is a good possibility of losing a job, for example, as layoffs happen all around us. But some part of us wants to hold on to the belief that difficult life events will happen to others, not us. Maybe it's a way to protect ourselves from worry, but humans are well practiced in the denial of reality.

During good times, we all try to imagine living through a life crisis. We try to imagine the difficulty in facing the challenges of a serious illness or job loss and coping during transition, maybe even working through the social stigma of being unemployed. We might picture ourselves as somewhat prepared for the emotional and financial stress.

However, no matter what we imagine, it's impossible to be ready for the reality that sinks in on the last day at work, or the day after that, and especially the day after that. People who leave an organization experience shock, just as we all do in the face of any sudden loss. The long commute home, finding the right words to explain to family and friends, trying to make sense of what happened—it all seems unreal.

The next morning is often the biggest surprise, as one wakes up ready to begin a familiar morning routine, only to be hit by the stark realization that there is nowhere to go. A kind of post-traumatic shock sets in: surprise, panic, and blame, and back through the cycle a thousand times again. How can this be? How did this happen? How could this happen to me? Others, sure, fine ... but not me!

The reaction is similar to the moment when we learn that a loved one has passed. Even when we know that someone is sick and not getting better or that he is elderly and time is short, nothing truly prepares us for the event when it finally comes. An emotional response occurs that we cannot really prepare for. The telephone call that brings the message or the tap on our shoulder from the boss stuns us. I can't believe this is really happening!

## Witness the Shock

A first step in starting over is simply to witness the shock—to observe your reactions to the events at hand as you begin a path toward acceptance. Whatever you feel is okay, from a mild annoyance to absolute terror, from irritation to dark anger, from confusion to total bewilderment. All of these emotions are typical and normal reactions to a traumatic event.

Losing a job, especially unexpectedly, may make us feel as if we are going to roll into a fetal position and just die. We will all die some day, but certainly not from embarrassment or from surprise about being let go. The truth is that many, many people are experiencing similar transitions these days.

Also important to know is that the strength of your reaction will ebb and flow, and the intensity will lessen over time. Through care of your mind, body, and spirit, you can find a way through, just as thousands of others have. Tools contained in this book and in many other places will help you get through. You will be okay.

A good and very practical first step in the face of shock is to remember to breathe. It may sound overly simplistic, but taking deep breaths in helps to make your mind clearer and letting deep breaths out releases the stress in your body. Try it—just breathe in and breathe out. Let everything go for a moment and help your body relax.

You may want to begin a regular meditation practice (as suggested in Chapter 12) to really focus on reducing stress, but breathing is a good start. Remember to breathe.

## Let Go of the Old Vision and Dream Again

Some of the shock comes from expectations we have about how life will turn out for us. If we commit to a partner for life, divorce is something that happens to other people—that other 50 percent of the population. We are committed. We imagine ourselves always having a strong emotional bond with our mate, working hard to create a life together, building some financial equity, and maybe even expanding our family. We imagine ourselves having fun together in the future, retiring together after we are done with our work lives, after we have built that financial equity (collected our stuff). We might be enjoying our adult children and maybe even their children, celebrating our holidays and family traditions. We might see ourselves traveling together, enjoying the rest of our lives.

One of the biggest shocks of a divorce is the loss of that vision and that dream. A black hole is left. What will the holidays be like now? Will I be able to get by financially? Will I be retiring alone? Traveling alone? There is no longer a common picture for the future or for the evolving pattern of life. Now what do I do?

The same is true for our work lives. We start out eager to learn and to get ahead, to work hard, to build career equity. The unspoken assumption about work life is that if we are honest, work hard, do quality work, and commit to our employer, we will in return achieve success, create a little security, and ultimately be happy. We expect an occasional promotion and steady pay raises, maybe even bonuses.

Mostly we anticipate a pattern of moving up, of always working toward something better. Anchoring this illusion is a dream about the end of our careers: In our final few years on the job, we will be a respected elder in our work community, things will slow down a little, and we will go out with accolades and honor. If not a gold watch, we will carry the pride and esteem that is symbolic of success.

One of the biggest shocks of being forced out of an organization early is the end of this vision of success. There is more to prove; we are not done yet. The dream of the gold watch is not about the gold watch, but it is about going out on a high, and when we leave early, that dream is lost, it is unfulfilled.

That is not the way the movie is supposed to end.

## Believe You Will Be Okay

But then life moves on. People find ways to start new dreams and new journeys. Maybe it is a chance to renew ourselves, to remember what values are important to us, and to capture a brand new vision. Maybe it is not about racing back to another large corporation, but to live an entirely different life, maybe a chance to really make a difference.

The journey of transition benefits from faith—a belief that life will work out in the end. If you dare to believe the movie of life can have a good ending, then life can be even better. Any loss is just a chance—in disguise—to start over.

In my coaching practice, I wish I could collect a Loonie for every time I have heard, "You know, I should have left months ago. Why did I stay so long?" [An acknowledgement here for my Canadian friends. A Loonie is slang for the Canadian dollar.]

Who we think we are as human beings somehow gets intertwined with what we do at our day jobs. Our status and rank at work become our self-perceived position in life. We become our jobs, and when our work isn't going well, our lives don't go well. When we become our jobs, our self-concepts become tied to our self-perceived success.

We convince ourselves that staying in our current jobs is our only reasonable path. Starting over and doing something else would be just too difficult. At least, right now it would be too difficult. We don't see any other apparent or easily accessible paths through life, and sometimes it is easy to assume there aren't any.

In reality, life always holds many options for us.

## Look at Life Again

In reality, we live in a world of abundance, and there are many options or paths to happiness. One great joy in life is experiencing some of the ways through life that we didn't expect and some that we didn't even know were there. It is always healthy to keep our heads up and to examine all of our possible options.

Are you stuck? Ask yourself: Am I truly enjoying the path that I am on today or am I placating myself to cope?

People sooth or numb themselves in many ways for a variety of reasons, including to avoid difficult and painful questions about their life choices, to avoid being conscious about the present, or to avoid the emotional discomfort of acknowledging the need to take a different life path.

Besides the classic ways of anesthetizing with alcohol and drugs, people watch too much TV, eat too much food, compulsively browse the Internet and check e-mail, get lost in "analysis paralysis" instead of deciding, and the list goes on. If you are stuck, leaving might be a renewal for you that is long overdue. If you were feeling stuck in your work and were asked to leave, maybe life did you a favor. Life made a good decision for you. We cling with everything we have to life's passageways, but sometimes we just need life to kick us through.

Believe that you will be okay. If you want to, you will be okay. The message here is about the great thrill of taking step changes in life and learning the mindsets that lead to success through the transition and onto the next leg of the voyage.


"Challenge is a dragon with a gift in its mouth.
Tame the dragon and the gift is yours."

—Noela Evans
Author, *Meditations For The Passages And Celebrations Of Life*

# 3

## Committing to Growth

"I am always doing things I can't do; that's how I get to do them."

—Pablo Picasso

### Letting Go of Clarity

Brennan Manning tells an enlightening story about Mother Teresa in his landmark book, *Ruthless Trust: The Ragamuffin's Path to God*.[4] In 1952, Mother Teresa had started her Home for the Dying, a free hospice for the poor in Calcutta, India. John Kavanaugh, who is a Professor of Ethics and Philosophy at Saint Louis University, traveled to Calcutta to work with her at the hospice for three months.

Dr. Kavanaugh had been thinking about ways that he could spend the rest of his life and, in part, came to Calcutta in search of his answer. In his first meeting with Mother Teresa, she asked him, "And what can I do for you?" Kavanaugh requested that she pray for him, and, in turn, she asked what he wanted her to pray for.

Reflecting on his search for answers about the future, Kavanaugh pleaded with Mother Teresa to pray that he find clarity. Brennan Manning recounts their conversation:

"She said firmly, 'No, I will not do that.' When he asked her why, she said, 'Clarity is the last thing that you are clinging to and must let go of.' When Kavanaugh commented that *she* always seemed to have the clarity he longed for, she laughed and said, 'I have never had clarity; what I have always had is trust. So I will pray that you trust God.'"

Clarity of the future is one of the first things that is lost at the start of a life transition. To build on the advice of Mother Teresa, letting go of a need for clarity is one of a number of mindsets that are critical for moving ahead with our lives during major change. Losing an anchor from our past means that life will be chaotic for a time, and the quicker we accept the chaos, the faster we can move ahead with our lives.

The challenge is to replace clarity with trust. Whether you have found trust in your God or not, the trust required at this juncture is faith that there is something good waiting for you out there. You may not find it immediately, but it is out there for you. Trust is the raft to the other side of the river.

The issue of trust is really about a choice we are forced to make at a *wall*. Fundamentally, we can choose to search for future success while being stressed out and worried, or we can search for future success with a little peace of mind. When we hit a wall in life, peaceful success depends on building our growth as a person. It is a wonderful time to start with a commitment to take a leap in the capacity to deal with life and whatever it brings, to build our threshold for coping with anything that might happen.

Maybe the bigger scheme of things—the plan created by the consciousness behind this universe—is to face a series of obstacles that provide an opportunity for growth. Maybe the only point in the end is that we do grow and that we learn our life's lessons while we are here. And with any luck, we can grow with grace. Whatever sandbox we play in, bumps and challenges await us. We don't really have a choice about that. Our choice is more about the joy we experience along the way.

## Commit to Growth

Everything happens for a purpose, often a purpose that we cannot see at the time. One purpose of any significant life event is to learn lessons—lessons about ourselves, what we are made of, about our character as humans. Those lessons in turn build our capacity to handle even more the next time. Our future security is within us, not in a next job or a new career.

The challenge is to become a learner in life instead of a knower, because knowers get rigid in their ways—a trait that is not adaptive to life change. A young sapling that can bend in the wind, compared to an old oak that is strong but inflexible, will survive better in a storm. And these days life is bringing storms.

So an important first step is to learn the thinking, the mindsets, that will allow us to grow no matter what happens. Commitment to a mission of personal growth starts inside of us, not outside. It starts with an assumption of *personal accountability*: We need to understand *how* and *why* we create the outcomes we get, to accept accountability for them, and to learn ways to increase our capacity to deal with whatever comes.

Accepting personal accountability for growth is particularly challenging when we're stuck in anger and blame. When someone gets separated involuntarily from an organization that he or she has sacrificed for, it is very difficult to get beyond the injustice of it all. People do get treated unfairly in organizations, especially those managed by people, because people make subjective decisions. Yes, that includes all organizations!

Decisions are made quickly under pressure, and often employees who are let go never learn the whole truth. In our litigious society, organizational managers perceive a risk in telling the whole truth. In all honesty, there is a risk, and effective human resources professionals are left to use the tools and strategies for letting people go that they know are legally safe.

Given that reality, it's important to get over it fast and to move ahead. If you were treated in a way that violated your legal rights, then go ahead and find justice. But no matter what, move ahead beyond the blame, for your own sake, and begin the process of discovering your next step. Life is way too short to get stuck in bitterness. When an organization lets someone go or an employee decides to leave on his or her own, it is an opportunity for EQ (emotional quotient), not just IQ.

So a foundation for successful transition is starting with a commitment to personally grow from the experience. What are the factors that help us learn what we need to, and what are the learning "disabilities"? One perspective is that the truly critical elements of this equation are embedded in our framing of the events—the way we choose to interpret what has happened to us.

And we all know the result. A person who is able to heal emotionally from a difficult past and show up during interviews with a positive point of view will come across much better than someone who is hanging on to anger or frustration. Even when we think we are hiding negative feelings, when we think we are doing a good job of faking it, our true feelings come across. They become evident in either our body language or in subtle inflection, maybe even in ways we can't consciously detect.

The right way of thinking and feeling will help us find that next opportunity; and even if that doesn't, the transition is a lot better experience. Being stuck in negative emotion ultimately never helps us get the results we want.

Here are some mindsets and beliefs that can help in transition:

- I will focus to control what I can and not worry about the things I cannot control.

- I will let whatever happens in my future be okay.

- I prefer to have faith that this will all work out in the end.

- I want a tolerance for ambiguity, as life will be chaotic and unclear for a time.

- I want to let go of any negative emotions, whether they are justified or not.

- There is a purpose in this life event, even if I cannot see it right now.

- There is a new role for me to play out there, even if I can't see it yet.

- I am me, I am not my job or my role in any organization.

- I am going to learn a lot from this experience!

- I cannot go back to the past, only into the future.

- This is a world of abundance, not scarcity.

- If I end up with less in some ways, I will have more in other ways.

- If I can create a clear and compelling vision, I will find my way.


## A Mental Game

*"Business is a mental game"* is one of Todd Sheppelman's quotes that any of his people could recite back to him when times were difficult. And times got tough a lot when he was growing his company's business, during a challenging economic stretch, to over a half-billion dollars in annual sales. His lone customer was the former home of José Ignacio Lopez, one of the fathers of aggressive purchasing practices: General Motors.

Todd is a *car guy* who still likes to cruise in his mint-condition, 1969 Chevy Camaro Pace Car convertible. He is one of the regulars on the annual Dream Cruise through Detroit's suburbs—a showcase event for one of the finest collections of restored cars in the world.

He began driving some of his father's '50s and '60s collector cars to weekend car shows at age fourteen, and soon after his first muscle car to high school in central Illinois, at least until his school's drivers' education teacher frowned on the practice. Automobiles were in his blood at an early age, and he thrived in an industry that these days takes as much mental and emotional muscle as car muscle. But then has always liked difficult challenges.

Todd was always a *favorite son* in the companies he worked for, moving from one promotion to the next. Early in his career he had worked for General Motors, who paid for his MBA at Stanford University. From there Todd was off on a series of one- to three-year assignments across three organizations in the United States and Europe, each with a corresponding move up. Life seemed to come easy.

In 2004 Todd was promoted to vice president at Visteon Corporation where he managed their global automotive components business with General Motors. He handpicked a team of professionals and then drove a turnaround strategy for Visteon's product line with GM. They grew the business from $175 million to $500 million in three years, and their profits soared. His people loved working for Todd, who was a natural leader. He was always demanding, but fair and an open communicator. He was also on a roll.

Three years later Visteon let Todd go. As a supplier in a shrinking domestic automotive industry, Visteon suddenly had too many vice presidents at the top. Waves of additional workforce reductions were already in the works at the company, but the move was so sudden and completely unexpected.

Todd was in shock at first—he had never left a job other than by his own volition, and suddenly he was "on the street." With the domestic automotive market wilting, finding another position at his level was going to be difficult. He started on a nearly sixteen-month search that would prove to be one of the biggest challenges of his career.

Once again Todd stood out—not because he was smarter than the many senior executives looking for work—but in the way he looked at his journey. He created a clear vision for success. He kept a positive outlook, never doubting that there was a good position out there for him that would eventually come. He networked with everyone he knew. He joined a support group of leaders on the same path and at one point had several dozen search specialists looking for him. For Todd this was just another life challenge, and his mental approach was going to make the difference.

Todd sold one company on his abilities and readied himself to take the position as their general manager. The CEO then became critically ill and was forced to stay bedridden, too sick to consummate the deal. For Todd that was just another obstacle.

Another company in Kansas City offered Todd the position as their general manager following several rounds of intense interviews. While he was on his way home, the company called and withdrew their offer. They were concerned that Todd would not make a long-term commitment to the company by moving permanently to Kansas City. Just another obstacle.

Finally Todd's psychological persistence paid off. After more than a year of searching for the right position at the right company, he got three offers to choose from as president or COO. He was hired as the North American president of another global automotive supplier, where a few months later he was promoted to the position of Global CEO. He didn't have to move from his home in Michigan, so every year, he can still drive his '69 Camaro at the Woodward Avenue Dream Cruise.

His vision had come true. Todd created exactly what he had dreamed of and had gotten even more than he had planned. The game of starting over is a mental game too.

## Coping with Fear

If one of the primary goals of life change is to learn and grow, the biggest learning disability is fear. During major transition, fear can slip into our lives in insidious ways. After a life experience such as losing a job, many lie awake at night ruminating through all of the negative possibilities: *Will I survive financially? Do I still have what it takes to succeed somewhere else? Am I too young/too old? Is there another job out there for me? What will my friends and neighbors think of me?*

Fear takes us into survival mode as we constantly scan the horizon, imagining possible dangers. The corpus callosum, which are the nerve fibers that connect our right and left cerebral hemispheres in our brains, quits working. Our brains work half as well (our dominant side takes over), our creativity decreases, and we begin to look for *safe* alternatives. We play not to lose—to avoid risk. We jump to convenience and security at a time in our lives when the biggest opportunities might be waiting just around the bend.

One form of fear is worrying about the future. If creating a clear vision and focusing on what we really want is like praying for positive outcomes, worrying is like praying for what we don't want.

Of course when someone leaves a good job, finances are almost always a concern. Contrary to common sense, it helps to let go of worries about money. Don't get me wrong. All of us would like to find personal fulfillment, but most of us would like to have personal wealth *and* fulfillment too.

But worry about money during major change locks people up in fear and creates a desire to jump at the first opportunity, whether it is the right career move or not. Money worries create a tendency to accept less, and life is too short. If you are willing to trust, the money you need will follow.

The challenge is to focus on the present moment, not to focus attention on the past or to worry about the future. There are a variety of stress management and psychological techniques such as yoga, meditation, systematic desensitization, and the deep relaxation response. Others find strength in spiritual growth practices like prayer. Stopping worry is easy to write here and really, really hard to do. But trust in the future is the kind of thinking that gets people through difficult times.

## Let Whatever Happens Be Okay

Sometimes they're planned, and sometimes they're not—either way the big shifts in our lives are still difficult. Whether one is involuntarily let go, voluntarily leaves, or retires, the next step is a big one. The change is normally a significant emotional event; therefore, an effective response to change requires emotional intelligence.

In outlining his Nine Principles for Conscious Living, Bill Harris defines a comprehensive model for finding success and peace of mind in any phase of life. The nine principles are a study in personal accountability, understanding the outcomes we create, and in assuming responsibility, not blaming factors outside of our skin. [5]

His first principle, an early step in moving to more conscious awareness, is Let Whatever Happens Be Okay. The point is that our emotional suffering or any experience of negative feelings like anger, frustration, anxiety, guilt, irritation, annoyance—any negative emotion—is a result of our resistance to the way things are. This is not an endorsement of apathy or of just accepting the way things are. It is about changing our *needs* to *preferences* and realizing that reality is what it is. If we get locked into the way things *should be*, and in fact things are not that way, we are signing up for some emotional pain.

It is important to always work toward our goals and life aspirations. If we get focused on what we don't like and don't want in our lives, instead of focusing on the vision we *do* want, we are destined to let life's obstacles and challenges become too great to overcome.

Low emotional intelligence sucks away the energy we need to take the next big step in our personal growth.

One example that Bill Harris uses in his talks is the very worst situation imaginable: someone learning that he or she has a short-term, fatal illness. The choice is really about either getting to acceptance of your fate and living every day of life to its fullest before passing, or getting stuck in grief and living a sad life and then dying. You are going to die either way. The choice is about the life that you are going to live in the meantime. It is the same lesson that Eugene O'Kelly taught us in *Chasing Daylight*.[6]

The same principle is true when you lose a job. Chances are you will not get the job back. The job has been lost. The best option is to accept what has happened, to make it okay, and focus all of your energy on the next step. Someone who makes this choice is going to show a better face when he or she gets that first job interview.

Another option is to get stuck in anger, blame, bargaining, and depression, to remain irritated and indignant, and consequently lose the energy needed for real success in the next step.

A similar phenomenon can happen to retirees. Their public face can say that life is wonderful, there is no stress or pressure, and they can do whatever they want. Privately, some retirees rehash old hurts; they remember unfair turns in career progression; they rethink less-than-ideal severance packages and curse downturns in organizational performance that lessen the value of stock options or retiree benefits.

Sleeping in and having fun never quite fills the painful hole left by the loss of a real sense of purpose. Big life change is hard. It's often difficult to find the point in going on.

## Wisdom and the Steps to Renewal

An important element of navigating transition is planning—creating a new, compelling vision for the future and outlining the steps to get there. But renewal of yourself is not only a left-brain, logical, task-oriented adventure; it's a rekindling of energy as well. A critical aspect of this journey is renewing your spirit, to capture the vigor needed to go on, to come alive again.

Many resources can assist in a job search and with resume writing, networking, and even planning for retirement. But there is less acknowledgment of the emotional roller-coaster ride you begin.

We already have all of the wisdom and the archetypes to guide us through any transition in our lives. We know in our hearts, as well as our heads, about the epic of loss in life, about the dip, and then the story of the phoenix rising from the ashes. Knowing the story and how it is supposed to unfold is far different from experiencing a real-life vortex of change. It helps to remember the steps in the voyage and also to be reminded that there are lots of reasons for hope and that this is a world of abundance.

As a first step, you need to understand the patterns of change and the emotional cycles that are certain to follow. Then it's important to get clear about the sequence of steps to move forward again, from healing to focusing on a new vision. The following chapters are sequenced to assist a life traveler in understanding the steps in the trip and to create a personalized path forward.

No matter how difficult the work of personal growth, it helps to remember that there is always a path to peace of mind and joy in your life. One element of a healthy spiritual life is a belief that, in the end, life will work out. It will. If you want it to, it will.

A reflection on the steps toward personal growth: You will know a lot more about the world around you in one year, in ten years, and certainly in twenty years. The biggest challenge in finding your future direction is your mind, knowing what you know, and blocking new possibilities from view. So start with a beginner's mind, not a knower's mind.

If we are still around as a species, we will know a great deal more a thousand years from now. And yet you have all of the wisdom you need to know the way right now. You simply need to listen to the messages that are all around you right now.

"And the day came when the risk to remain tight in a bud
was more painful than the risk it took to blossom."

—Anaïs Nin

# 4

## The Cycles of Growth

*Autumn*
Living is hidden within dying.

*Winter*
The winters will drive you crazy
until you learn to get out in them.

*Spring*
Nature teaches a steady lesson:
If we want to save our lives,
we cannot cling to them,
but must spend them with abandon.

*Summer*
In the human world
abundance does not happen automatically.
It is created when we have the sense
to choose community.

—excerpted from Parker J. Palmer[7]

### Life Happens in Cycles

Over time, we come to observe that life, like the seasons, plays out in cycles. In life we experience good days and bad days, positive stretches when we grow, and hard times when we cocoon.

Life has its ups and downs. After a time of living in a positive phase, events turn south for a while. If we get through the difficult times, life tends to get better, at least for a while. And so on ...

We are born, we grow up, and in the end we all die, even though we don't like to think or talk about it much. Yikes—none of us is going to make it out of here alive!

Paul Steinhardt and Neil Turok took this notion to a whole other level in their book *Endless Universe: Beyond the Big Bang*.[8] The Big Bang theory currently stands out as the most popular scientific account of the history of the universe. The conventional premise is that all matter and energy was infinitely compressed several billon years ago and suddenly exploded, expanding out to fill the known universe. Cosmologists over the last hundred years have conducted several experiments that seem to support the theory; in fact, they observe that the expansion of the universe is accelerating.

That's no surprise to those of us who feel as if time is moving faster every day.

It is difficult for the human mind to grasp the concept of infinite time, maybe because every life cycle that we touch seems to have a beginning and an end. Plants in our gardens bloom but then shrink away in the colder months. Every tree starts as a sapling, and when it is fortunate enough to survive the early years, it grows tall and strong. Older trees that have already completed their life cycles stand naked with no bark, as habitats for birds, or perhaps ready to be harvested.

Every pet lover understands that the price of bringing a new puppy or kitty home is that their life cycles are relatively short. At some point we are required to let them go.

Over our lives we build relationships with others, and inevitably we suffer the grief of loss. Even our earth and our sun started at some point and presumably will fizzle out.

The human soul may be an exception to our experience of life cycles, but an invisible veil limits our vision and keeps us from completely understanding the future after this life.

Steinhardt and Turok proposed a new theory of cosmology that supports the notion of infinite time, a cyclic explanation that suggests the Big Bang is true, but just one step in a series of major events. The authors suggest that there is no beginning to time and that the Big Bang is simply a transition from a previous chapter that they characterize as a "Big Crunch." While their theory is yet to be validated with scientific research, Steinhardt and Turok's assumptions do offer an explanation for little understood phenomena such as acceleration and "dark energy," the force that is used to explain expansion of the universe.

In other words, Steinhardt and Turok propose that the Big Bang is not the start of the universe, but simply one phase in an endless sequence of big bangs and big crunches, the expansion and then compression of all energy and matter. We are in an endless dance of creation.

Maybe when our souls leave this world for the next, we will know the answers to these questions for certain. As of today nobody knows how to see with confidence into our longer past or our future.

We do know, however, from studying the patterns of our own lives that they are played out in cycles. Life is a series of chapters and transitions, and each chapter begins, lasts for a period of time, and then ends in transition to the next. In a time of rapid change the chapters seem shorter, and the transition constant—what author Peter Vaill called the "permanent white water" of life today.[9]

Some contend that this pattern of human chapters and transitions continues until a final chapter of life on earth: death. Others believe that our last life chapter here on earth leads to a transition to a next and even better life. Maybe we'll find out some day.

## The Growth Curve

Navigating the turbulence of change is made easier through an understanding of the cycles and stages of the change process. Several models describe the process of moving from one state of existence to the next, but my favorite has always been the growth curve.

The growth curve is a model that describes the phases of growth in any living system. It can be used to better understand the sequence of birth, growth, and death in a product life cycle, or of an entire organization. The growth curve helps to understand nature from the tenuous start of a new tree sprouting from an acorn, to a tall oak, and finally to a shiny new floor. The model describes the phases in a person's life and the times he or she learns something new, grows to become proficient, and then later learns an even better way. Life is full of these cycles.

It's one thing to have an intellectual understanding of the process of change and quite another to experience life change firsthand. The thrill of a new beginning and the pain in loss both overshadow the significance of any theoretical construct. But understanding can help too. At least someone can know that what he or she is experiencing is normal and expected. Feeling emotion in transition is a natural facet of life, and our feelings define a lot of what it means to be human.

I learned about the growth curve from George Ainsworth-Land, a futurist who proposed his version of change as transformation theory. Ainsworth-Land was a member of a small team that was asked by AT&T to help beat a lawsuit filed by the Justice Department, which was trying to break AT&T's monopoly on the U.S. national phone service. He helped to convince AT&T to quit fighting the federal government and to concede by spinning off the "Baby Bell" companies, the entities that served as the regional carriers. The future was not in holding on to the past, but in growing with the rapidly changing telecommunications industry.[10]

As noted earlier, AT&T had mixed success in renewing their competitive cultural genes, but they learned some valuable lessons in the inevitable transition of organizational life.

Various models describe distinct phases of growth and change, some with five steps and others with seven.

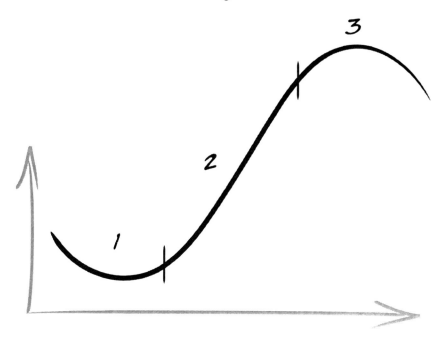

**The Growth Curve**

George Ainsworth-Land's growth curve has three phases including 1. Formative, 2. Normative, and 3. Integrative. In the simplest terms, every living entity defines itself by early life patterns, then grows and strengthens if those patterns are successful. Finally, at a breaking point, the rules for success change, and early patterns don't work anymore. The life cycle ends. The growth curve represents growth (vertical axis) over time (horizontal axis).

The growth curve describes the cycle of a new product that innovatively fulfills a market need, then grows in sales as the market responds, and finally fades away or combines with other, newer, and better products. The curve can also describe the macro view of an organization's life cycle as it moves from an entrepreneurial start-up, on to fast growth and finally to a plateau, ultimately to obsolescence. It can also be used to describe one of several micro-cycles in an organization's existence. As innovation creates the start of a new cycle, the new way catches on, then ultimately fades as a new idea takes its place.

The growth curve can tell a story as simple as a stalk of corn that starts as a single kernel, grows, and eventually is harvested. Or it can help us comprehend the emergence of bio-technology in global agriculture.

The growth curve is an excellent model for understanding the stages of human growth, from birth and infancy (formative), to physical growth and complex learning (normative), and finally to the end (integrative). We don't like to talk about it too much, but ultimately each of us will reach the end of our growth cycle, and we will die. Can't someone change that principle before it's too late? Probably not.

It's the cycles of our human lives that will be the focus here. We go through many growth curves in our lives, each with the start of a new growth spurt or a new skill or simply a new way of looking at the world. While our lives can be described in terms of a single curve, it's understanding all of the smaller life cycles and their interconnectedness that lends insight into the mosaic that comprises a human life.

## Phase 1: The Formation of Something New

In Phase 1, the formative phase, life starts. If the basic conditions for growth are present, life will begin to flourish.

Phase 1 paints a picture that describes the infancy of a child, a first day at school, a first job out of school, or a first date. In many ways it can be a painful period of time, at least emotionally, as we struggle to find a formula for success, or a replicable pattern that will lead us to success, to growth, to becoming whoever we are destined to become.

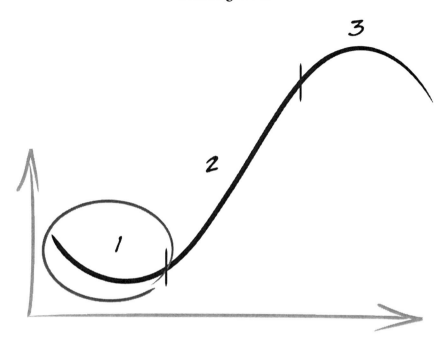

**The Growth Curve: Phase 1**

Phase 1 has several classic qualities. For some reason we just assume that our progress from day one will be straight up, that life will get better every day as we move off into the future. Interestingly, just the opposite happens. Our plan aims high, but the curve of progress regularly goes down before it goes up. When young children decide to pull on the courage, or the blind faith, to take that first step, they typically stumble in their first try.

You probably don't remember what you were thinking at your first step, but if you had been able to think, I am sure it must have been something like this: "Okay, this crawling thing is starting to get boring and I have a lot to do today, so I guess it is time for some serious ambulation. I think I'll just start walking around like my mom, starting today. Alrighty then, here we go ..."

Ouch! By the grace of God, you probably can't remember what happened with that first step. If you could, you might never have taken another risk your whole life. But if you were like my kids, some part of your face was quickly introduced to the floor. You might have taken the rest of that day off, perhaps learning your first lesson in procrastination. Walking could wait until tomorrow. At some point you took another step, maybe with the support of a parent or a sibling, but you kept trying to take steps and eventually found the rhythm of it all. The one foot in front of the other lesson: why do we keep having to learn that lesson over and over?

So when we learn something new, we often start on a downward trend before we learn, before we grow. Think back on all of the times that you started to learn something new and how you weren't very good at first—talking, reading, running, riding a bicycle, playing sports, playing a musical instrument—the list goes on. Almost everything we learn is like that, unless it is very close to something we already know. Kids just seem to accept that, and with a little encouragement, they keep trying to learn new things, maybe failing at the start, but they keep trying.

Somehow when we become adults—and decide that we never want to be embarrassed again—learning new skills and starting new behaviors gets harder for us. But if we want to continue growing, we have to get comfortable being uncomfortable.

Why does our performance tend to get worse before it gets better in Phase 1? It seems as if our minds and our bodies want to stick with what we know already, to stay in our comfort zones. The classic learning curve describes a principle of slower learning and mistakes early on, with effectiveness and efficiency coming only after lots of practice. It is as if our psychological immune system wants to pull us back to the past.

Companies or social agencies that create new services or new products go through the same trough of performance in the formative phase. Organizations that are either starting up or spinning off as new ventures create a vision for future success and then plan to go straight there. What always happens, of course, is that all of the factors that inhibit instant success offer full resistance from the beginning. An organization goes into what Seth Godin, the best-selling author and marketing specialist, has coined the *dip*.[11]

## Grow or Die

For lots of reasons, life gets worse before it gets better. It's just a natural part of the cycle of life. A real predicament arises when people use that dip or lack of immediate success as an excuse not to start new life adventures, or not to stretch and learn something new. Ongoing success in life requires regular growth. There is no staying still. In a world that seems to change faster over time, the only choices are to grow or to go backward—to grow or die.

Starting a first job is a good example of the formative phase of the growth curve. As we learn a new job, we inevitably make some early mistakes, which we craftily attempt to mask. Somehow it would be comforting to believe that this principle isn't true for brain surgeons or commercial pilots, but everyone gets better with practice. Fortunately mentoring and simulation can provide experience through the early learning cycle, until we are ready for real life.

Examination of the early, Phase 1 stage of an entire organization follows the same patterns. As an entrepreneur begins the process of creating a "start-up" company, his or her hopes are focused on the moon. Anyone who has had start-up experience talks about two simultaneously intense emotions. First, there is the exhilaration of not having any limitations, which is so freeing. *Anything is possible!* Especially for those who have come from larger, bureaucratic organizations. Finally, no more wasteful procedures and paperwork— the work can finally be done the right way (which incidentally is *my* way). *Why in the world didn't I do this a long time ago?*

The second, parallel emotion is absolute terror. *What if this venture doesn't work? I am going to at least lose my house! Why in the world did I do this?* If a new entrepreneur has come from a larger enterprise, where he or she was insulated from the harsh realities of the marketplace by a critical mass, working in a start-up is living "close to the street." Despite the fear, however, being an organizational pioneer can be like coming alive again.

Real life is like that: a weird blend of excitement and fear, coming at us all at once. It's the same way we feel when we jump off on a new career.

Another classic archetype that emerges in the formative stage of a new organization is that everyone plays a number of roles or "wears a lot of hats." On Monday and Tuesday an entrepreneur might be developing a new product and then be out selling it on Wednesday. On Thursday and Friday he might be trying to produce enough product to fill a new customer's order and on Saturday afternoon delivering the order in his van. When survival is at stake, people do just about whatever it takes.

If we were to take an anthropological microscope to examine the pattern of behavior in Phase 1 of a growth curve, we would see a lot of confusion and chaos.

The start-up phase is all about finding that replicable pattern, a formula for success that can be repeated over and over. For an organization, the goal is all about finding a product or service, a value proposition, that the marketplace will latch on to and pay for. For a social agency, it means discovering a service that truly improves people's lives by providing what they really need and want. The actual product or service that customers buy is often different than originally planned, and the race is on from the start to find the formula for success before cash or budget runs out.

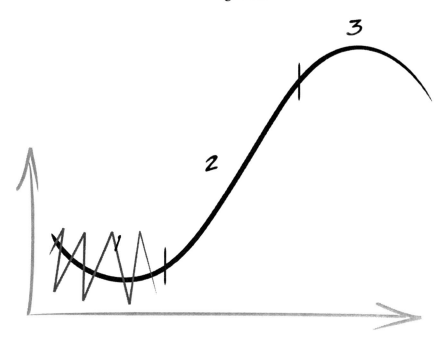

**The Growth Curve: Searching for a Replicable Pattern**

For an individual, the replicable pattern for success might be how well she learns to live by the established values of a new workplace—how well she fits in the new culture. It might be an engineer learning new customer-relating skills in a new marketing job or a salesperson learning the disciplined protocol of a product development process. In that first job out of school everything seems to change, from social etiquette to expectations for work hours. Learning something new means trying out new behaviors to see what sticks and what the new culture criticizes and rejects.

And the world seems to continue to spin faster. The U.S. Department of Labor reports that, on average, today's employees hold more than ten jobs by the age of forty-two![12] More than 50 percent of employees age twenty-eight to thirty-two stay with their current employer for less than a year, and more than 85 percent of those same workers stay with an employer fewer than five years. There is a lot of change going on in this new world.

People who change organizational cultures after several years in one environment often come to a new employer with a rigid set of habits that are hard to change. It's difficult to fit into a new culture, but someone who is open-minded and resilient can do it by being observant, by coming in with a beginner's mind, and by learning the new replicable pattern, the new habits, that win in the new workplace. It's the confusion and chaos of Phase 1 that people feel during these transitions.

Most of us can look back on a time when we were not successful starting something new in life. In his book *Failing Forward*, John C. Maxwell has collected a highly entertaining set of stories about very successful people who all experienced failure on their journeys to achievement.[13] It seems as if anyone who reaches a high level in his or her career started a company that didn't turn the corner or got fired from at least one job. While others who came before us might have worked a single job throughout their entire careers, it is more unusual these days, and employees move from job to job, and even from career to career.

In other words not everyone survives Phase 1. Some people don't fit into any work culture or don't have the acumen to be successful. Some jobs and careers don't suit some people. Organizations and people are not always a good fit. Some people choose not to fit in, and some just cannot learn fast enough to adapt to a different environment.

That might mean getting cut from a sports team, or not making the cast of a school play. About half of marriages in the United States don't make it past the honeymoon phase. Anyone who works for a while will find a job that is not a good match.

Seth Godin list seven reasons someone might quit before he or she becomes the best in the world at something:

1. You run out of time.

2. You run out of money.

3. You get scared.

4. You are not serious about it (committed).

5. You lose interest or enthusiasm or settle for being mediocre.

6. You focus on the short term instead of the long term and quit when the short term gets too hard.

7. You pick the wrong thing at which to be the best in the world (because you don't have the talent). [14]

The same principles apply to start-up, Phase 1 organizations. There are a lot of debates about the statistics, and mergers and acquisitions of start-ups certainly cloud the picture, but many new businesses do not succeed. Some say that rate follows the Pareto Principle, i.e., only 20 percent succeed after five years, or in other words, 80 percent of businesses fail within five years. Professor Scott Shane of Case Western University suggests that in the 1990s, across industries, the correct figure was closer to 55 percent failure after five years and 71 percent failure after ten years. [15] Whatever the exact number, a bunch of companies that start up don't last very long.

There are a lot of life lessons in Phase 1 for someone who is starting over in life. For one, it is okay to quit if you are quitting "strategically." For example, a new job really doesn't fit or, in the case of a start-up company, spending more means following bad money with good. However, for someone who has been in a comfort zone for a time, starting over will always mean some chaos and emotional discomfort.

If we are determined to avoid the pain that new challenges naturally offer up, we will stop ourselves from learning new directions. The risk is quitting too soon. As Martin Luther King was quoted as saying, "So often the darkest hour is that hour that appears before the dawn of a new fulfillment."

What can we learn from a romantic who upon divorcing his sixth wife proclaims, "I want to find a woman who truly understands me!"? Yes, chances are he doesn't truly understand himself, and that perfect partner is not waiting out there. Whether you believe in reincarnation or not, life does offer a series of lessons that you can stay to learn, or you can move on down the road and learn those lessons later. You could even skip the lesson altogether. We might as well stay right where we are and learn the lessons at hand.

Adults work hard to remain emotionally comfortable. But starting over in life is always difficult, whether it is about being let go from a job, leaving a job and starting a new one, retiring, getting a divorce, or whatever. So the biggest lesson of all may simply be to get ready to struggle and to know, like all of the cycles of life, that it is just for a time. And not incidentally, there is a lot to be learned in a life of stretching out.

Sometimes we choose to quit by choice, but often we fail at something new because we are not conscious of the unwritten rules for success in a new environment. We become blinded in new circumstances by what we already know and hold on tightly to being knowers, instead of becoming learners. But if by chance we do discover a replicable pattern for success, a formula for achievement, we earn the right to turn the corner and head up the growth curve. We earn the privilege of moving on to Phase 2.

"The world is changing. The old ways will not do. It is time for a new generation of leadership."

—John F. Kennedy

# 5

## Into New Growth

"Let go of the illusion of impending stability.
Nature never settles down, and we are not going back to normal."

—Todd Sheppelman

**Leaving a Safe Harbor**

Dave Doster tells the story of his wife Cindi's reaction when he came home and told her about his new career: "What! I thought you were going to get a job?"

Dave had taken the plunge that many of his corporate brethren only dream about. He was leaving what appeared to be a safe and secure job at a large company to start his own consulting business. He was getting ready to start over.

For Dave this was a big deal. He had worked at Ford and Ford-spinoff Visteon for more than twenty-five years, most of that time as a fast-track executive on his way up the ladder. Dave is a natural leader whom people want to follow, just by being himself. He has an instinctive, relaxed way with people, an unpretentious senior executive, who builds trust quickly. His people at Visteon fought to stay on his team instead of accepting promotions to higher-paying positions.

Dave had paid his career dues with stops in engineering, manufacturing, and international operations. He became a vice president and an officer of the company when he was promoted to lead Visteon's first sales organization. He was being groomed to do it all, and at one point was asked to manage all of Visteon's global marketing, sales, and service for the Ford account, an organization with over $16 billion in revenue.

When the automotive industry began to plateau, Dave's career leveled off too. He had never been one to quit. He had learned a steady work ethic at an early age, working by his younger brother Dan's side on his grandfather's Ohio farm. On a small family farm, some days the sun shines and some days it rains. In some years the crops are good and, in others, not so good. But no matter how difficult the challenge, the *farmers' code* says a good farmer stays the course. It is a matter of loyalty and faith—if one works hard even when times are tough, the Lord will provide. He always has.

So Dave stayed the course for a time but knew that he had unrealized potential. All of the classic concerns about starting his own business came into play: *I have only five more years to get to my thirty-year pension—shouldn't I stick it out? How will I pay for health insurance? What about the vision that I've had for twenty-five years?* There were a lot of reasons to stay put, but a lot more reasons to actualize the dream and to grow. Dave left the nest and started his own business.

As soon as Dave left, his new business took off. He was finally reaping the rewards of years of specialized experience, cashing in on his years of know-how and wisdom. In typical fashion, others followed him, attracted by the chance to work for a genuine leader who cared for his people as much as his results.

Besides the financial rewards that followed, Dave began to reframe the world of work. A large number of senior managers are discovering that as jobs fade away in a shifting economy that starting over doesn't mean finding another comparable corporate job. With those who have value to add, the world is one of abundance with a million ways to stay engaged in the world of work. The game is no longer about staying loyal to one organization or even industry but about discovering the many meaningful ways to contribute and make a great living. Dave has gone on to become the CEO of another start-up with limitless possibilities on his horizon. He took the leap and won.

If we are fortunate enough to find our way through the natural resistance that always exists in the formative phase of a new growth cycle, if we find a way to win, if we are able to cross the dip, we begin the ascent up a new growth curve. At that point, we step into Phase 2, the normative phase of growth.

## Phase 2: Taking Off

The normative phase is a time of rapid growth, and for many this phase is the most exciting part of the cycle.

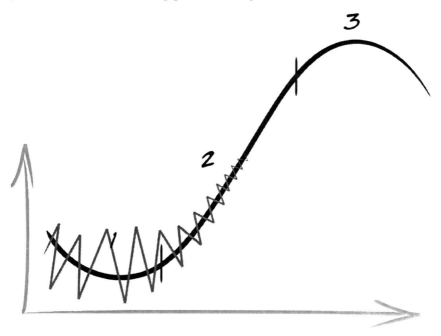

**The Growth Curve: Reducing Variation**

Phase 2 is all about building on a newfound formula for success, a new repertoire of achievement. At this point the goal is all about reducing the variation in Phase 1 and becoming more efficient and effective in executing. Phase 2 is about implementing a new formula for success and doing it better and better over time.

We know we have hit Phase 2 when we are "hitting our stroke."

The normative phase begins a period of defining who we are and who we are not. If acting a little crazy works to get someone's attention in middle school, one might get good at becoming the class clown. If one has been receiving attention for academic achievement, she might begin a lifelong commitment to learning. Based on the replicable pattern that begins to be successful, we drive a stake in the ground and decide which behaviors work and which behaviors don't work.

The paradox, of course, is that as circumstances change over time, whatever formula did work, probably won't work well at some future point. Our fundamental values and beliefs—the things that don't change over a lifetime—are an exception to this principle. High school teachers may not be as tolerant of a class clown, and then the consequences get serious. A studious academic may miss out on future fun if her life isn't balanced. Unknowingly, we plant the seeds for future failure by defining a tight formula for success. But we don't usually think about that at the start, because Phase 2 is all about refining our formula and doing more of what we do well.

Human beings have an incredible capacity to learn complex behaviors and then become proficient without conscious thought. Watching an accomplished musician playing piano or guitar reminds us that human fingers seem to move faster than the impulses from our brains that trigger them. Interpersonal skills that define a great leader become second nature, and the supportive behaviors of a great teacher grow to be automatic. The artistry of a master woodworker seems to sprout from pure intuition.

Any novice who walks onto a manufacturing floor for the first time is often overwhelmed by the complexity of sights and sounds. How then does an expert machine operator understand by tuning in to subtle noises, movements, or vibrations that adjustments are necessary?

My mom was incredible when I was a child. My parents had eight children altogether, the handiwork of devout Catholic parents back in the day. As a stay-at-home mother, my mom somehow kept track of all of us at once. It took support from the older siblings and perhaps some fear of God on our part, but remarkably she kept us all alive, well fed, and generally healthy. I can still see my mom simultaneously cooking on the stove, helping us decide what to wear to school, packing lunches for school, and bending over to help the little ones tie their shoes, without even thinking. Committed people are capable of extremely complex multitasking when necessary.

Tiger Woods, arguably the best golfer in the world, reinvented his stroke not only once, but twice. Can you imagine being the best in the world at what you do and then deciding to go back into a new learning curve, to let go of slightly less-than-perfect habits in search of the perfect? And then doing it all over again?

Likewise, Michael Phelps returned home from the 2008 Olympics in Beijing after winning a record eight gold medals, the most by any athlete in a single Olympic games. After a break to rest (and some would argue a little too much fun), he came back to serious training and decided to try a new freestyle technique, letting go of the approach that had made him the best ever swimmer in the world. Why? He wasn't chasing his past goals any longer, and his new goal, of getting faster in the sprints and the shorter races, required a new approach.

Top performers understand that even when things are going very well, there is always another step toward perfection. Being the best is a constant game of reinvention of one's self. This mindset rails against the belief that "if it ain't broke, don't fix it!" There is no *good enough*, and no resting on one's laurels.

Phase 2 feels so good, which is one of the traps of the normative phase. Emotionally we want to stay in our comfort zone, which is a place where we are very good at what we do. Only the best performers and those truly committed to growth understand the truism that Jim Collins, the author of *Good to Great* taught us: "good is the enemy of great."[16]

## Arrogance

An early normative phase in an organization is marked by rapid growth and prosperity, as the marketplace "gets in line to buy a better mousetrap" or a better product or service. While the start-up phase is marked by a free-wheeling, entrepreneurial spirit and creativity, Phase 2 is known by standardization and discipline in procedures and processes. The goal is to get more and more efficient and to reduce variation.

Phase 2 requires a different kind of leadership than Phase 1, and many entrepreneurs don't successfully make the shift to a world that reduces spontaneity. Most true entrepreneurs are committed to avoiding the kind of bureaucracy that they left in the past when they took the risk to start something new. But without the development of standardized processes, an organization will never reach its true growth potential. So it is not an issue of good or evil; it's an issue of selecting the approach that works best for the life phase.

Great organizations have a knack for ending a new product (or service) development phase, and then standardizing processes, while at the same time constantly trying to invent new ideas. It's not an either/or proposition, but a both/and choice that leads to ongoing market leadership.

Individuals are the same way. To grow, we must continually get better at our core competencies while constantly searching for new mindsets and skills.

The ego raises its ugly head during the normative phase of growth.

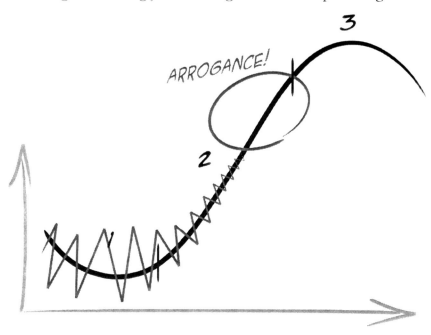

**The Growth Curve: Phase 2 Arrogance**

At some point up the curve we become arrogant. Organizations become arrogant, and the people in them equally so. This ego factor is one thing that makes it so difficult for us to let go of a past that no longer works for us.

This is especially true when life demands that we become a beginner once again, starting over with a new cycle of growth. We long for the days when we were the best, at the top of our games. It's easy for us to believe that we have earned permanent respect or that we have become entitled.

In yet another of his remarkably insightful books, *How the Mighty Fall*, Jim Collins describes his research findings about organizational factors that determine success or failure in Phase 2.[17] Collins describes the stages of demise of previously great organizations as they begin their descent, or choose to reverse it, beginning in late Phase 2:

- Stage 1—Hubris born of success: People become arrogant and consider their success an entitlement, forgetting about the underlying factors that created success in the first place.

- Stage 2—Undisciplined pursuit of more: Success is seen as more growth, which occurs faster than excellence in execution.

- Stage 3—Denial of risk and peril: People ignore the signal of demise and blame reasons outside of themselves.

- Stage 4—Grasping for salvation: People look for instant, silver-bullet solutions to their problems. Companies search for a "knight in shining armor" to save them.

- Stage 5—Capitulation to irrelevance or death: Leaders give up hope.

Unfortunately, many large organizations place less emphasis on the renewal required to thrive in a changing environment and focus instead on systems and structures designed to maintain control. Production systems, physical buildings, organizational hierarchy with clearly defined degrees of status, policies intended to standardize, and regulations all become an end in themselves.

While all of these systems are intended to maximize success, collectively they can conspire to stifle improvement and slow the renewal necessary for organic change. Mature organizations can become immune systems that spit out innovation.

Individually, as we become more proficient learners, we enter into Phase 2 of our physical, our intellectual, and our emotional growth curves. We get good at what we do. At just about the time that we are starting to feel good about ourselves, however, we tend to fall into a couple of human traps. First, we think that we are doing well because we are unique in our intelligence, at least a lot smarter than those before us. We easily delude ourselves into thinking that we are doing well because we are better than others or are, in some way, superior.

Second, we think that because we are so good at what we do we are going to continue improving, we are going to stay in Phase 2 forever, and things will always get better and better. Finally, we have it all figured out!

This illusion is similar to the opposite scenario that when things are going poorly for us, they will continue going south and will get worse forever. In the middle of a recession, it seems as if we will never pull out. When we are out of a job and looking, it seems as if we will *never* find another one. When things are going well, we can't imagine that they will ever get worse. Why would they? We are *really good* at what we do!

While getting quite good at something is wonderful, it is equally important for us to be constantly reinventing ourselves, all the while remembering our core competencies. This constant renewal means getting out of our comfort zones, learning new skills, getting even better at old skills, and constantly growing in some way. Even if a person's one thing is brain surgery or rocket science and he is the best in the world, over time the techniques and the technology will change; so learning remains a requisite skill.

Getting stuck in any single thing, no matter how good one is, makes starting over all the more difficult.

## Hitting the Wall

No matter how good we get, at some point, every living thing hits a wall.

A wall is an indicator that even though we might still be very good at something, it is no longer good enough for continued success. A wall is a breakpoint—a moment in time when the rules for survival change.

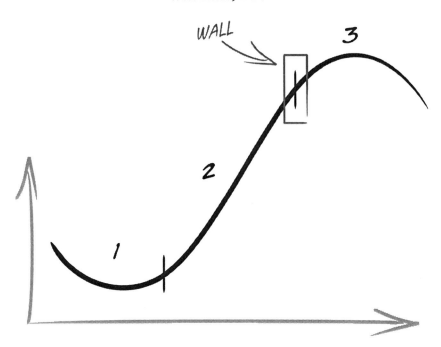

**The Growth Curve: Hitting the Wall**

Consumers expect more from a product or service, and organizations expect more from us as employees. Sometimes our old behaviors just don't work any longer in a new setting. Customers want something new and exciting. Trees simply reach the end of a genetically predetermined life cycle. Human beings reach the end of their genetically predetermined life cycle. For one reason or another, every living system reaches the end of its time, and growth begins to plateau and eventually fall off.

My son Bill came home from middle school one day and proclaimed, "Eighth grade rules, Dad!" Now when I was in eighth grade working diligently at St. Rose School, trying to please some wonderful teachers from the Sisters of St. Joseph, the word *rules* meant something important, and I am sure my heart skipped a beat or two. But what Bill was actually saying was that eighth grade was simply a great time in life.

## Starting Over

In the United States educational system, eighth grade is the last year of middle school, which includes grades seven and eight or maybe grades six through eight. In eighth grade, the kids are typically the oldest students in the school, and with seniority comes several unspoken social privileges. The eighth graders are "King and Queen of the Hill," if you will, at the top of the social hierarchy. They decide what clothes are *cool* (if they still use that word) and what style of dress is passé.

The eighth graders get to decide what jokes are funny and what humor is childish, hardly sophisticated enough for eighth graders—and more appropriate for kids way back in seventh grade. Because there is often a big difference in physical development from ages thirteen to fourteen, the eighth graders are typically the best athletes in the school and are able to dominate mixed-grade sporting contests.

Don't cross an eighth grader on the playground, or you may be introduced to the meaning of "Hertz Donut!" [That's a quick punch to the arm and a taunting, "Hurts, don't it?"] I certainly don't mean to advocate bullying, but in middle school the natural order of the social caste system is at play.

I never truly understood the tricky mindsets of those eighth-grade girls. They somehow seemed to begin learning the secrets of older women at about the age of fourteen. Maybe it was ancient archetypes that finally surfaced in their consciousness, passed along from primordial goddesses, and then from generation to generation. As far as I know the Sisters of St. Joseph had secret classes with the eighth-grade girls to teach them the undecipherable thinking patterns of their mothers and older sisters. So I can't speak to the experience of my female friends.

But I can tell you this: the life of an eighth-grade boy was great. We were the best athletes and social monitors at the school, and those crazy girls somehow thought we were cool too. We were the most suave males around, I guess, at least compared to the snotty-nosed seventh graders. In retrospect, the truism that everything is relative seems to have a foothold in middle school.

All I had to do was save enough money from my paper route for admission to the middle school dance and then two ice cream floats at Miller's Ice Cream Parlor to qualify as a hot date. So what if my mom was giving us a ride to the dance? Nobody had wheels back in eighth grade, anyway.

So eighth grade was a wonderful time of life, at the very top of the social totem pole. After the nanosecond it took for these pleasant memories to flash through my mind, I watched my son's sparkling eyes testify to the same fundamental truth.

At that moment my mind raced ahead to his future, to his next year in school, surely to the harsh end of a wonderful dream—he would become a freshman in high school! I couldn't say the words out loud because Bill's brain was surely awash in alpha waves, relishing that special moment in his life. Let him have his pinnacle; let him enjoy every second. Next year, *everything* would change.

I am not sure what being a freshman in high school was like for you. Most people I know think back on those days as one of the toughest periods in life. While you could be at the top of the social heap one year, all of a sudden, there you were at the lowest low, the very bottom. Being a freshman must be life's way of showing us all what a wall is all about.

On the first day of high school, the newcomers are lost, wandering the halls and looking for their classes. Once they find their lockers, the lock combination never works right, at least not in time to make class. When someone finally gets into his locker, some upperclassman is sure to find delight in locking him inside, or maybe hoisting him up on top of the lockers, left to desperately call for help for someone to rescue him.

When I was an eighth-grade boy, the girls were all friendly, but by the start of ninth grade, it was pretty hard to get their attention: *Want to go to the dance on Friday night? Forget about it! I'll be home studying ...*

## Starting Over

*My mom said she would drive us to the dance if you want to go?*
*I would love to, but my boyfriend Brad is going to pick me up in his*
*Corvette after football practice.*

Oh, man, the dagger of daggers!

While last year, you might have been one of the best athletes. This year, heaven help you if you make the varsity team, because the play gets rough with the big kids.

Enduring a myriad of embarrassing experiences, freshmen are also likely to be the helpless recipients of torture that could make the Russian KGB blush. In my high school there were the classic high school pranks such as "Swirlies"—the cruel act of holding someone upside down and dunking his head in a flushing toilet bowl, creating a swirled look in the long-haired students of the day. (I have often wondered if those poor freshman in the Southern hemisphere had hair that swirled in the opposite direction.) If a swirlie weren't enough, there were always the aforementioned hertz doughnuts, wet willies, wedgies, atomic wedgies, noogies, Dutch rubs, and of course "kick me" signs taped to one's back.

There was so much to learn as a freshman. If that same creativity had been applied to school work, we all could have been done in two years. [This embellishment of reality in the description of being a freshman in high school is intended as a humorous way to describe a challenging time in life and not in any way meant to advocate hazing. Hazing is a dangerous and destructive practice.]

The rest of high school follows the classic growth curve cycle. By the time we are sophomores in tenth grade, we begin to gain confidence. At least we know more than those naïve, incoming freshman. Maybe we even gather a little swagger in our walk down the halls. By the time we become eleventh-grade juniors, we edge into the arrogance phase, and we become pretty sure we know everything. At least we know a lot more than our stupid parents. And by the time we become seniors in twelfth grade, we are insufferable. We become convinced that we are all-knowing and ready to survive on our own. We are complete adults.

Of course, the next year the cycle starts all over again, as we become insecure freshmen in college or start a new job, once again at the bottom of the social ladder.

So, we all promise ourselves never to go through an experience like being a freshman in high school again, not ever. The emotional scars we gather at this point in our lives keep people from coming back for high school reunions twenty, thirty, and even forty years later. *I didn't like those people much back then, why would I want to go see them again now!*

## Life Is Full of Walls

There are so many examples of hitting walls in our lives. In every case, it seems like a signal that our behavior from the past just doesn't work well enough for the next phase of life. Think about the Neanderthal tribes in southern Europe when they first comingled with modern homo sapiens, Cro-Magnon man. Many have hypothesized that the Neanderthals' lack of language and their small clanlike social structure didn't allow them to collaborate well enough to repel their new invaders.

Think about the Roman Empire and all of the walls they hit, including an overtaxed economy, religious conflicts, and new invaders like the Huns, whom the Romans were not equipped to fend off.

Think about the British and how they used to rule the seas and their colonies with their superior navy, and how their experiences in America started a gradual decline in global influence.

Think about your own life when you weren't ready for some new challenge because it was different from past challenges that you had conquered.

Sometimes the world seems to fall out beneath us, like when we are doing great work but the economy slows. You can imagine the plight of the world's best buggy whip manufacturer when people began to switch from horse-drawn carriages to automobiles.

American automotive manufacturers had the same experience when they tried to sell trucks and large SUVs after gasoline had rocketed to over $4.00 per gallon. The trucks and SUVs were great vehicles; it was just that the market dropped off. Same story for a lot of high-tech firms in 2000–2001, when new start-ups could no longer attract capitalization, and the markets began to demand commercial success. Things change all of the time in this crazy life.

During the economic recession that began in 2007 a lot of very high-performing people were let go from their organizations. One of the difficult mental and emotional challenges for those employees, at that economic wall, was rejecting the insinuation that they were let go because they were not performing. So many people were still great performers, but the opportunities that they had been groomed for were simply gone.

A master carpenter might not have work in an economy that discourages housing start-ups. Sometimes we hit walls because our behavior is not good enough for the next level. Sometimes our behaviors are not in demand at the next level. In any case the requirement is the same—we either figure out what the new conditions demand, and learn new behaviors to succeed, or wait and hope for a past reality to return.

## Our Choice at the Wall

Nature doesn't actually care how we feel about difficult change. Over time we realize that, while life can seem cruel, our journeys are a sequence of changes, of hitting one wall after another as we navigate through. We clumsily start new experiences, and if we catch on and like them, we get good at them for a time and become proud of what we do. We might even think we have finally figured it all out.

Then, for one reason or another, as soon as we think that we have life figured out, we hit another wall and have to start over again. Living is an ongoing series of interlocking growth curves as the world constantly asks more from us. Our choice is to continue growing or to go backward—to stop growing, to die.

Our choice at the wall is a choice of mindset.

- Will we see a wall as an opportunity to stretch and grow into something better, or is the wall a signal to go into survival mode and to hold on to the past?

- Is the wall an opportunity to play to win, to use all of our resources to take risk and grow, or a death knell that signals a need to play not to lose, to avoid risk, to lie low, to hunker down and just get through?

- Is the wall a reminder of entropy, that life is falling apart, or syntropy, that the forces in life are recombining to a higher order, to something better?

When we are starting over in life, getting ready to turn a new chapter, the answers to these questions make all the difference in the quality of the journey. Having the right mindset doesn't change nature or get rid of natural fear, but the way we think about change is a requisite tool in getting the courage to go on—to fight the battle. The way we frame the challenges at the wall is where we gain the capacity to move ahead and grow. We can change without growing, but we never grow without changing. And we never grow within our comfort zones.

We are good at dealing with change, so long as it is the same kind of change that we have always experienced. If it is new and different, we are going to struggle. We might as well plan on it and enjoy the ride. If we survived being a freshman in high school, we can do anything.

"Failure is only the opportunity to begin again more intelligently."

—Henry Ford

# 6

## The Vortex of Change

"I had seen birth and death but had thought they were different."
—T. S. Eliot

### A Vision for the End

When we look back on our lives, the changes we experience make sense. In retrospect, we can see the patterns more clearly and understand the bigger purpose of the changes our lives take us through. While we are hitting the walls of life, however, the changes are often surprises. In retrospect, the true surprise is that we would expect anything different from exactly what happens. Somehow when life is going well, we just assume that the good stretches will always continue and that life will just keep getting better and better.

When we imagine our final wall, our death, somehow we see the Hollywood version. There we are, old and gray, but somehow still physically attractive and at peace, with our family and friends around our bedside. While everyone around us is gently sobbing and proclaiming how we have profoundly and forever changed their lives, we fade off into a gentle sleep, never to awaken again.

I hope it happens that way for me and for you too. But in reality people die every day racked with pain, unable to breathe, alone, and without a chance to say goodbye. Sudden accidents happen, people die because they are sick, and some outlive their loved ones. This point of reality is not intended to be negative or depressing to anyone, but that's just what real life can bring.

Like every other moment that we are alive, we need to be prepared for any circumstance, to choose to be happy no matter what happens.

We typically imagine the end of our work lives in much the same way. There we are at our going-away party, getting that gold watch or at least some plaque or other symbol of a great contribution to the organization. Our coworkers are "roasting" us in jest but at the same time making testimonials about the difference we have made in their lives and the incredible contribution we have made to the organization. We *have* made a difference; we've left a true legacy that people will remember for years to come. Our work lives have mattered. Ah, thanks once again to Hollywood, it is a wonderful life.

Sometimes it happens that way, but currently, more often than not, it doesn't come close. The testimonial made by a senior manager working for one of my clients, a major oil company, comes to mind. The organization had decided for financial reasons to close a division of its operations and to transfer some of the employees to Houston.

The manager said, "*I gave my life to this place for almost thirty years. I worked through vacations and I missed my kids' games—I sacrificed my family for years. I was loyal to this company and look what I get back? I am being asked to move away from my home, where I have lived for years. I am being asked to give up everything I love.*"

At least he had been offered another job. The old, unspoken contract held that if an employee was willing to work hard, to be honest and to be loyal to the company, the company would take care of that employee, to be loyal in return. That silent, and yet implicit, agreement has changed in this world of constant turmoil and economic uncertainty. Many long-term employees work hard for twenty, twenty-five, or even thirty years for their companies, doing great work. Then they are forced by financial realities to leave. They have to start over. There are no congratulations, no retirement parties, no roasts, no kudos, and no testimonials, just a sudden and unplanned escort out the door by security.

## Rick Wagoner

Think about what life must have been like for Rick Wagoner. Rick was asked to leave his job by the President of the United States, Barack Obama. By the President!

Rick Wagoner was the Chairman and CEO of General Motors Corporation in March 2009 when the federal government began to exert influence in the U.S. automotive industry. GM was attempting to get $16 billion more in aid from the government after already receiving $13.4 billion in December 2008.

According to industry analysts, Rick Wagoner's removal demonstrated that the Automotive Task Force appointed by President Obama was serious about forcing GM to change more quickly and to send a signal that a more radical restructuring of the company was in order. The task force believed that required changes in GM would be difficult to make without significant changes in GM's Board of Directors and senior management. Rick Wagoner may have been the symbolic, sacrificial lamb in the process.

Imagine the experience from Rick Wagoner's shoes. George Richard Wagoner had grown up a smart student and gifted athlete in Richmond, Virginia. Things came easy to Rick and he excelled in life early. He was named "Best All Around" student in his high school class. He attended Duke University where he made the basketball team as a walk-on in his freshman year. After graduating from Duke in 1975, he attended Harvard Business School where he earned an MBA in 1977. After school he was recruited by General Motors, one of the largest corporations in the world.

Wow, life must have been looking pretty good, and it just kept getting better. Starting as a financial analyst in GM's treasury department, he moved up quickly through the organization, working on assignments in the U.S., Brazil, and Europe. He became President and Chief Executive Officer of General Motors in 2000, at age forty-seven—the youngest CEO in GM's history. He was promoted to Chairman of the Board in 2003.[18, 19]

Anyone who is driven to succeed in a large corporation knows that you don't get to the top without being brilliant, having some exceptionally good luck, and mostly being willing to commit your life to your work. You don't move to the very top of an organization like GM working 9-to-5; it means a lot of hours, seven days a week, thinking, eating, and sleeping work. It means a lot of missed school plays and kids' games, but hoping that work will settle down one of these days so life can approach normality. It means a great deal of sacrifice and a supportive family to make it all work.

But no matter how smart you are or how many hours you work, no one person controls the underlying economic shifts and markets. At the zenith of Rick Wagoner's career, the U.S. automotive industry shrank at an alarming rate after years of relentless competition from foreign transplants. He made a lot of progress in attempts to fix structural flaws in GM's business model by globalizing engineering, manufacturing, and purchasing. He improved quality and forged new agreements with the United Auto Workers Union. As sales fell, Rick cut GM's costs by reducing its workforce by nearly half.

At the same time, General Motors lost close to $80 billion, its stock plunged, and Toyota surpassed General Motors as the world's leader in automotive sales.

Could Rick Wagoner have done more? In retrospect, probably. He made changes at a deliberate pace, perhaps not quickly enough for the rapidly declining business. He also failed to tackle a fundamental issue that would keep GM from economic viability: retiree benefits including health care. He resisted the federal government's suggestion that the only true structural solution would involve bankruptcy. Surely employing his assumptions of the form a bankruptcy would take, Rick Wagoner's belief was that customers would never buy new cars from a bankrupt company.

Given his ownership of and history in the culture at GM, we wonder whether Rick Wagoner was capable of making enough of the drastic changes needed to forge an economically viable auto company. Maybe someone with little or no emotional attachment to the business had to take that step. More likely, by the time that Rick Wagoner took the helm in 2000, the decline had already begun in earnest. Maybe the decline actually began back in the 1970s, and it was too late for any mortal human to reverse, even with a full understanding of the direction GM needed to take.

Could you or I have been more successful? Probably not, but let history decide. Personally, I am just happy that far fewer people will be interested in dissecting the success of my career when all is said and done. Anyone who becomes a senior executive knows that the position is fragile and rarely long lasting. Subjective interpretations of a Board of Directors, fickle markets, political communities, and a myriad of other factors—being at the right place at the wrong time—can weigh in when organizations decide to select a new senior leader.

Rick Wagoner left his job at GM with enough severance pay and other compensation to ease some of his pain. Many of the souls from the bowels of the organization who were let go but still needed to work for a living fought a harder battle. But after such a gifted life of success, who would plan on the story ending that way?

Where is the gold watch? Where is the proud legacy? Life can bring any of us storyline twists that are impossible to predict. Despite our positive visions, unexpected endings require us to choose between holding on to bitterness or accepting our fates and moving on to start over again.

Among all of the alternative endings that can play out in our lives, the Hollywood ending is often not the one life serves up. We can pray that our jobs end positively and that we move right into something better—either a next job or a happy retirement. But that apparently is not always life's plan for us.

## An Old Curve Ends, A New Curve Begins

The rational thing to do when we hit a wall or see one approaching in our lives is to start a new curve.

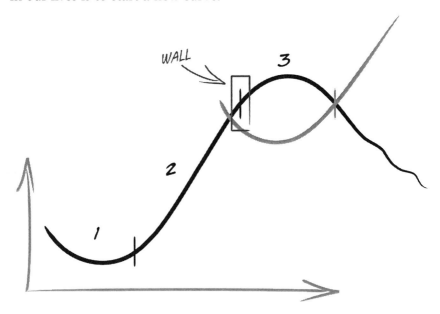

**The Growth Curve: Renewal**

At least that's the way we see ourselves, as intellectual beings: in control, letting go of past ways that no longer work, and continuously making leaps to better approaches to our lives and work.

We all know the formula—when we see that a past approach to success no longer works, we move to a new tactic. When we learn from a classmate or older sibling that Santa Claus doesn't exist, we stop writing letters to the North Pole and accept reality. When we move to high school, we simply grow up and act like the older kids.

If, at a young age, we commit to a partner for life, we give up our all-night partying and just stay home together, drinking tea and talking. When we welcome a child into the world, we immediately become responsible parents. When we lose a job, we forget the past, and just go out and get another one. It's as simple as that, right? If only it were ...

We understand this principle in concept, but these transitions are the essence of what makes changing from a past to a new way difficult. At this juncture, we enter the vortex of change. The vortex is the component of the growth curve that makes the model so dynamic and interesting. These times make our lives fascinating too.

Life is an ongoing process of trying to grow up, which is a task that never truly gets done. No matter how far along we get in life, there is always more to learn and more change to make.

The vortex of change occurs during the transition from one growth curve to the next.

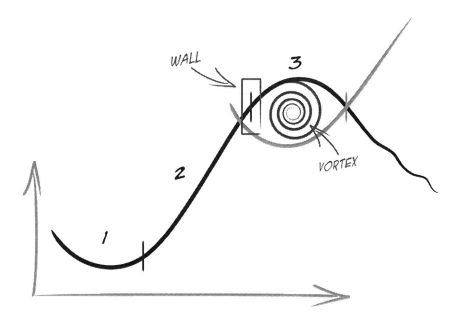

**The Growth Curve: The Vortex of Change**

A vortex is the span of life when a pattern for success in life begins to fade and a new pattern begins to emerge. The old way is going away, and a new way is starting. It is a period of death, but also it is a period of life renewing. The vortex is the time when death and birth become one.

The vortex tends to be a time of fear, and there are at least two fundamental sources of anxiety: First, we don't have a clear vision for where the new life cycle will take us. We are not sure if it is going to work out. In reality, eighth grade is not a perfect time of life, because growing up is hard to do. But at least it is a way of life that we know, where we understand the rules of the game, how to get by, and how to survive. When we become a freshman in high school, we're not completely sure we will ever be able to figure it all out again.

A number of my friends who have lost their jobs worry about the unknown that awaits. They sometimes look back fondly on their past jobs, and even though there were always lots of issues, at least it was a way of life that they knew. They knew how the system worked, how to get things done, whom to call when a problem came up, and whom to lean on for support. Those were the good old days.

The core of this concern about the future may be self-doubt, an apprehension of being able to succeed in a new system. *Will I still have what it takes?*

One evening at dinner after my son Bill had just finished kindergarten, he shocked the family with a dramatic announcement, "I have decided I am not going to first grade. I just want to go back to kindergarten next year!"

It seemed at the moment like such a mature decision, perhaps as if he had been doing some ten-year strategic planning alone in his room. I hadn't taken strategic planning during my one year of kindergarten, but what the heck, kids learn so quickly these days. Maybe he had been moved to the college preparatory track without my knowledge. But then I snapped back to reality and asked, "Bill, I am surprised. Why don't you want to go on to first grade?"

Without the slightest hint of a smile, Bill said, "My friend Geoffrey told me that kids in first grade know how to read, and I haven't learned how to read good [sic], so I'm not going!"

In other words, what if I get there and look stupid? What if I make a mistake in front of everyone? What if I am wrong and everyone knows it? What if I suffer the humiliation that comes from not being perfect from the first day on?

What if I get to the next growth curve and I don't succeed? It is the inherent fear of any entrepreneur, or of any of us starting a new course in life. There I'll be, a freshman in high school all over again.

My response to my friends who are looking for work is almost always the same: You are smart, and when you get there, you will figure it out. You will make some mistakes along the way, but you probably won't die from them, and certainly you won't die from embarrassment. You will do the same thing you did in your last job—when you get there, you will have the resources you need, and you will figure it out.

Easy for me to say and hard for any of us to do. Most of us are afraid of the unknown to some extent.

The second fear that makes the vortex a challenge is the fear of letting go of the past. People get locked into the ways things get done, in both conscious and unconscious ways. My good friend Patrick Edwards says, "The two strongest forces in the universe are first, gravity, and secondly, the force of habit." I am not sure. The force of habit may be stronger.

As creatures of habit, we tend to stick with what works for us. We have a desire to "go back home" to our comfort zones and the habits that we know. In the Revolutionary War, the British stuck with straight-line battle formations that had served them well in the past, but they were using old strategies in a new game, in guerilla warfare, where they were vulnerable to hit-and-run tactics. The U.S. learned some of the same hard lessons in Vietnam.

Many incoming high school freshmen try the same jokes that were funny back in eighth grade. Some new college freshmen are surprised when they can no longer plead their way to good grades and have to actually study for the first time. New parents find their parents' words spilling out of their mouths, automatically, like prerecorded script. *Don't make me pull this car over!* Our habits are what we know, and we become restricted in our ingenuity by our existing behaviors.

When an organization hits a wall, employees often revert to what futurist George Ainsworth-Land called the back-to-basics bump. In the back-to-basics bump, we do whatever we have always done in the past that worked for us. And when we see that those same behaviors don't get us the same results, we emit them harder and faster. We do what we have always done, but with more intensity.

This phenomenon can be observed in organizations when people begin to say, "We need to get back to basics, back to the things that got us here." While this approach can be helpful in eliminating unnecessary complexity, it is often a signal that the organization is reaching back to its past.

Unfortunately, the replicable pattern for success that worked so well in the past may not work in the future. The conditions, the market, the times, and the customer need may have all changed. Ironically, we want to get better results by doing the same thing over and over.

The fear of letting go of the past seems strongest when we don't see new, alternative behaviors that will create success. Likewise, that anxiety is strong when people who won big in the old system may not do as well in new conditions. The common denominator is human beings who, despite all of the flaws of the past, knew back then how to win or at least how to survive. When the future is unknown, we wonder if we will ever win again and if we have what it takes to survive.

In the face of letting go of what we know, in the face of the unknown, it is tempting to retreat to the safety and security of the past. When we don't have a choice to stay—we are outplaced, downsized, let go, fired, or given an early retirement—we have to move forward and not freeze up.

It's important to give up the past. That doesn't mean to throw out the baby with the bath water, to give up everything we know, but simply to come to acceptance that things have changed and what worked for us in the past may not work in the future. That is one of the sacred principles of the growth curve: the formula that created your past success, that got you where you are, will not be the formula that gets you to the future.

## Burn the Ships

Sometimes it is healthy to cut off any avenues for retreat. When Spanish Conquistador Hernando Cortés landed in Mexico on the shores of the Yucatan Peninsula in 1519, one of his first commands was, "*Quemar las naves!*" or translated to English, "*Burn the ships!*"

Cortés was not only dismissing the authority of the governor of Cuba who had ordered the expedition, but he was removing any opportunity for retreat by his men. His goal was to capture the great treasure of the Aztecs, and he demonstrated his commitment to move ahead into an unknown future by eliminating the chance of going back to safety.

The purpose of building personal commitment when we hit a wall and a vortex of change is to give us the energy to get through. In a state of fear and stress, from letting go of the past and an unknown future, we tend to go into survival mode. Our inclination is to protect ourselves, to remain safe, to slow down until we understand the terrain, and to be cautious. The phrase that I think best captures our tendency in the vortex is to *play not to lose*. When people play not to lose at work they remain in silence, waiting for someone else to take a chance in speaking the truth. The self-perceived risk of making a mistake is too great.

When an entire organization is filled with people who play not to lose during transition, it can become paralyzed, diminishing its chances of the very survival people crave. These human dynamics slow an entity during change, at a time when it needs to innovate the most. The irony is that, by silent consensus, employees in an organization cast their own eventual doom. Both nature and free enterprise reward those who innovate and take risk—who try new things.

The trouble with playing not to lose when searching for a next career, job, or life is that we are never on top of our game. We are our most creative and resourceful selves when we feel safe and supported, when we are just being ourselves.

The real peril is not being at our very best when we show up for that first job interview or attempt to make that next sale to our customer. The goal is to get through the vortex and fast. The dynamic that always slows us down is fear. As MIT professor and author Peter Senge said, fear is a learning disability, because it keeps us from learning new ways to succeed in the future. Getting through a vortex fast means letting go of the past and the fear and moving ahead.

## Wang

Wang Laboratories was founded by Dr. An Wang and Dr. G.Y. Chu in 1951. The company went through several growth curves in its history. Before venturing into personal computers, Wang produced typesetters and calculators, but they made their name in the 1970s and 1980s manufacturing word processors. In the transition from electric typewriters to personal computers in the office, Wang dominated the market in word processing.[20, 21]

After its introduction in 1961, IBM's electric typewriter, the IBM Selectric, controlled the lion's share of the market—close to 75 percent. Among other innovations, the Selectric used a novel typing ball that allowed a user to change fonts. Even though the typing ball had been invented years earlier, IBM's ability to make changing fonts easy with high-quality results was radical. The IBM Selectric signaled the start of desktop publishing. It created a widely accepted, replicable pattern for success.[22]

When Wang began to sell their word processors in 1976, which were actually multi-user workstations with individual terminals and processors, they introduced a product that was a step-change improvement in user friendliness. The ability to fix a typo or change a word or an entire sentence without retyping the entire page was a breakthrough. The improvements in efficiency enticed every office with the right budget to get a Wang word processor.

The software for early personal computers was not especially user friendly, and spread sheet applications like Lotus 1-2-3 were more advanced than word processing software. So Wang continued to dominate, perhaps with a touch of Phase 2 arrogance that is common when any company becomes the market leader. To IBM's credit, their introduction of the IBM Personal Computer, along with the marketing prowess to make IBM and "IBM compatibles" the industry standard, showed everyone that they were not ready to roll over and die.

To the point of this story: Wang clung to the formula that made them successful—stand-alone machines that were capable of word processing but not the many other applications that made the PC popular. While PC word processing lacked the capabilities of Wang at first, popular programs eventually emerged, such as WordPerfect and Microsoft Word, which has become ubiquitous.

In the meantime, Wang made a strategic decision not to become IBM compatible, an act tantamount to giving in to the enemy in An Wang's mind. It is rumored that An Wang plotted a chart of projected growth that indicated that Wang Labs would overtake IBM in the 1990s. Wang's business faded, eventually culminating in bankruptcy in 1992.

Hanging on to past patterns in a rapidly changing world amounts to planning for eventual failure. Henry Ford's declaration, "You can have it in any color you want, so long as it is black!" to describe the Ford Motor Company's commitment to simple, low-cost designs for automobiles is famous. His quote came at just about the same time that General Motors began to introduce a variety of design elements, including colors, into their cars.

GM simultaneously captured market share that became larger than Ford's, a gap Ford never closed. Both General Motors' and Ford's ongoing commitment to large trucks and SUVs, because of the short-term profit advantages in the early 2000s, may have cost them both dearly when market conditions changed.

There are many proposed reasons that we pundits offer for the decline of the domestic U.S. automotive industry. It's easy to second guess, and really difficult to reverse, declining trends that began in the 1970s. Large organizations that become constrained by their systems and procedures, to the detriment of systematic innovation, always fade over time, no matter how powerful they once were. Strengths from the past become weaknesses when conditions change. Nature can be cruel.

While it might be difficult to see today, the new global market leader Toyota is surely defining their formula for success in a way that will catch up with them in the future. While it may be hard to imagine, their success formula will become their formula for decline unless they are able to constantly adapt and innovate. What will the Chinese and Indian auto manufacturers teach us when they hit the markets with their full force?

So the pattern continues and the cycles are inevitable. The lesson for individuals—even though letting go of past rules is hard and future blueprints are not yet apparent—is we need to move ahead to grow. This doesn't mean that we should ever let go of our fundamental values and visions, but we need to be ready to let go of anything that is transient or temporary, which is just about everything else besides our values. When we start to hang on, we stop growing. The principle is to grow or die.

The time we spend in a vortex of change can be very difficult, both intellectually, trying to understand what our new curve will look like, as well as emotionally, letting go of our comfort zone. Successful navigation through change is as much an emotional choice as a rational, intellectual choice. Success is about emotionally letting go of the past and, at the same time, embracing a new future we have yet to see. Is that the definition of faith, of trusting that the future holds positive promise even when it has yet to show up for us? One key to triumph in a vortex, the times when we are starting over again in life, is remembering that life will be good again, and likely even better.

The way we think about our life transitions is a critical aspect of the journey. It is important to see the world recombining to a better state, not falling apart around us. We need to see that life is simply changing to something better. It is the difference between seeing entropy all around us and seeing syntropy, a reconnection of elements to a higher order. And if we are willing to see life that way, it will get better. It has been happening in nature for all of time. It's just hard when it is happening to us.

One of the key life lessons that Seth Godin reminded us of in *The Dip* was that doing anything in life worth doing includes some obstacles and challenges along the way.[23]

Didn't we all know that already? Why do we have to learn some lessons over and over? Extraordinary gifts come to those in life who are willing to push a little longer than others. We tend to settle for less than we are capable of when life gets difficult as we let go of comfortable ways from the past or avoid an uncertain future.

John Quincy Adams said, "Patience and perseverance have a magical effect before which difficulties disappear and obstacles vanish."

These principles are easier to see in others' lives than they are in our own. It's easy to keep going and to be flexible when the change doesn't affect us. Watching someone who is talented play basketball on television looks easy, but getting out there on the floor is a whole different matter. Some of those players are extremely tall, and years of practice make it look easy. It's not.

These days, we are definitely in the permanent white water.

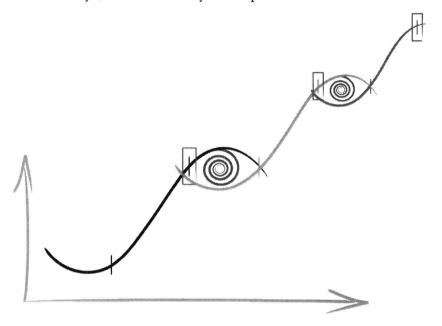

**The Growth Curve: Ongoing Transition]**

The Phase 2 normative cycles are becoming shorter, as we jump from one vortex to the next. As technology progresses and, at least figuratively, the world spins faster, life for people in our society is constantly in transition. The skills for coping with change are all the more important to survive, and the emotional capacity to let go and move quickly can make the difference in success.

Change has always been a part of life, but this doesn't seem like evolution. It is more like revolution.

But we're not the first people alive to experience radical change. The period from 1950 to 2000 was one of unusual stability in the bigger picture of civilization. We can't be hampered by the *illusion of impending stability*—that is, that soon things will settle down, and we can get back to normal. These just might be the good old days right now.

We can't expect that life will settle down, and so we need to get better at dealing with whatever life hands us. We don't have a choice to stop it or to slow it down, so we had better get good at coping. Chances are we are all going to be starting over several times.

> "When people shake their heads because we are living
> in a restless age, ask them how they would like to live
> in a stationary one, and do without change."
>
> —George Bernard Shaw

# 7

## The Stages of Grief and Letting Go

"All changes, even the most longed for, have their melancholy;
for what we leave behind us is a part of ourselves; we
must die to one life before we can enter another."

—Anatole France

**Kenny Weller**

As a nine-year-old boy entering fourth grade in St. Rose School, I began to cross paths with some of the older students. As I walked into the school entry on that first day of the school year, there he stood, the coolest guy I had ever seen. Kenny Weller was a sixth grader, and as we all know, by the time someone gets to sixth grade, he has it all together.

Kenny wore spotless white jeans with creases as straight as an arrow. My mom knew not to buy me any white jeans—the knees would have been perpetual green stains. Kenny's Madras shirts were ironed and radiated all of the colors in the rainbow. He spoke with the deep-voiced confidence that only a sixth grader could muster, one who clearly knew the ways of the world. He was tall, a gifted athlete, and for sure a ladies' man. Kenny was my sixth-grade role model, and I couldn't wait to grow up and know it all too.

In the fourth grade, sixth graders seemed to be able to do anything. At nine years old, two years of age difference, in either direction, makes for a big gap in developmental stage. So there are big differences, especially when the majority of your universe is contained within the walls of an elementary school.

Likewise, in fourth grade, parents and other adults simply knew everything. My life growing up on a farm in the Midwest probably inspired more naiveté than was found in the average fourth grader, but a belief that adults know all about the world is not uncommon.

From my perspective at nine or ten years old, our elders seemed to share a common and yet secret script, known only to them. They know how everything works. They can drive and buy groceries—*anything* they want! Adults know how to get money at the bank, fix the plumbing, teach school, and converse with other adults. They can do anything.

It's only later in life, in our rebellious years, that we discover that it is a ruse, a story that is propagated by the adults to fool us, to get us to follow blindly. Of course as kids we accept the story. Still, we become incensed that adults have been supporting the illusion that they are all universally competent. Mysteriously, when we reach our rebellion phase, adults know hardly anything at all!

Nonetheless, the fundamental mindset sticks deep inside us, even after rebellion. We carry an assumption that we are going to finish school and learn everything we need to know. Then we will get a good job and live out our good lives, using all we have learned. We will have fun and, at last, have it all together ourselves.

Once we are adults, we will also know it all. We'll have families and friends, maybe even some kids, with whom we can share our secrets about life. While it is far, far off into the future, one day we will die peacefully in our beds, with white hair, and our families at our bedsides. And that's about it. Life will go fairly smoothly once we get to be adults.

We don't have to get far into adulthood to realize that knowing it all is always around the next bend. That steady state of adulthood that we imagined is far from it. Life is full of ups and downs, of good cycles and bad, of starting over, again and again.

One of the fascinating things about growing up is our *surprise* that real life is littered with walls and vortexes. There are constant and ongoing revelations bursting in the minefield that life serves up. Why would we have expected anything different? Why would we expect that it will ever settle down? It's just the opposite.

Kenny became a good student and a sports star in high school and then went on to college. I followed him to the same university where, early on, he served as my mentor, helping me get started on the right foot. From there Kenny went to law school and finally moved back to our home town and became a respected attorney. Very predictable.

At some point the journey stopped making sense to Kenny, and all alone one night, he took his life. The world lost a wonderful man that day. Those of us who knew Kenny still miss him, his flat top, his ever-present smile, his quick handshake. Sometimes life just doesn't make sense. It's never what we plan.

The point that doesn't make sense is our expectation that life should be any different from exactly what it is. It's our assumptions that make change difficult. It's our resistance to reality that makes the truth so hard to accept. The sooner we get to acceptance, the easier life gets.

We are never going to get it all together, and if we ever do, you know what that means. The next wall is not far off.

## Loss and the Cycle of Grief

When life's circumstances force us to start over, the changes we experience can be like an emotional roller coaster. People often jump from feelings of bewilderment and confusion to anger, to sadness, to deep frustration, and back through the cycle again. After a long time of being successful, maybe even a lifetime, if we are no longer in control of what life brings to us, it's easy to slip to the negative side of the emotional barometer.

Even though we say to ourselves that life has its ups and downs, we still expect to get what we want. We become used to receiving the rewards that our past behaviors have produced. This is especially true after a long run of Phase 2 success. Even in a life sprinkled with significant loss or disappointment, we never seem to get used to major life change. We want to be in control of our destinies.

We don't mind change. We just don't like being changed.

- *My boss let me go. I gave my life to this organization, and look at what I get!*

- *My company restructured and it looks like I didn't make the cut. I don't know what else I could have done.*

- *This economy is bad and getting worse. The work is drying up.*

- *I can't take this job anymore—I have to get out of here!*

- *My company edged me out the door, but I'm not ready to quit. I have too much gas left in this tank.*

Whatever the circumstances, it hurts to experience a major life loss. But we are never alone. Even when people seem to be on the ideal path early in life—the perfect grades, the perfect mate, the perfect job, the perfect little house in the suburbs—it's pretty difficult to grow too old without a difficult loss. There are significant emotional events waiting for all of us on the path of life, no matter how good things seem early on.

Understanding the cycle of grief and how people respond during loss lets us know we are okay. Given our human nature, our response is predictable and normal. Grief is how we are supposed to react; it's a common part of getting through transition. Grief is a vital part of the bigger cycle of life.

## Faith in the Outcome

Brian Anderson knew that his work was slowing down as he and his teammates went through the motions of looking busy. His business unit hadn't sold any new products in some time, and the work in the pipeline was gradually slowing to a trickle. As a program manager with years of experience, he could implement a new product development cycle practically with his eyes shut—efficiently, smoothly, and all with a keen sensitivity to customer satisfaction. The programs just weren't coming through like they used to.

In his well-developed, rational left brain, Brian knew that his company couldn't justify keeping him on the payroll forever. And yet in his emotional right brain, he knew that he had been a loyal employee, committed to the company and the customers he served, and he performed as well as anyone. How could they not notice his dedication and understand the passion he had in his heart for the customer? Sure, the economy was slowing, but look at all of the good work he had done and all of the sacrifices he had made for the organization. Surely management had noticed and would stay loyal to him too.

Brian prayed to God that He would protect him and allow him to keep his job. With two sons in college, the time was just not good for starting all over again. While he had dreamed of moving on to a more challenging career that would allow him to stretch and grow again, the action seemed premature. Not now. Some day, when things settled down a little more and when the economy was back to normal. That would be a better time to make a change.

At some point the inevitable became obvious. The economy was not improving fast enough, the company was not doing well, and there were no new customer programs on the horizon. The organization went through a series of restructurings and shrank again and again. It was just a matter of time. Brian knew that his days were numbered and eventually even learned through the grapevine when the final day would come. He went to work that day with the anticipation that it was finally going to happen. This would be his last day. He knowingly watched as human resources and security personnel walked up to his desk with boxes to pack his personal belongings. This was it.

The final day didn't seem like a big deal when the time actually came. Brian had already taken most of his possessions home. No big deal. His goodbyes had already been said. It was a common event in the company in those days, so there was no shame in being let go. It was a relief, in a way, when the moment finally came. Brian was free to do whatever he wanted for the rest of his life, and who knew what great things the future might bring?

And then Brian got to his car in the parking lot. He threw his box in the back seat, got in, and turned on his car. He sat there for a moment, just to reflect, as he was driving away from work for the last time. Wow! The magnitude of the event hit him. This was it. This was really it. *I can't believe that this happened to me!*

The drive home was a blur. Walking in from the garage with his single box took a lifetime. What would he say to his wife when he got through the door? *Well, today was the day ... It's a good day to start over, I guess.*

Brian walked down the hall to his son's room, where his two boys were watching television. With all of the gravity of the moment catching in his throat and a face drained of expression, he made the announcement that after many years with the same company, he was unemployed and would be looking for a new job.

*That's tough, Dad. I'm sure you'll do okay. But could we talk about this later? We're right in the middle of this movie!*

Well, maybe it really wasn't the end of the world. Life goes on. If the kids weren't going to be freaked out, maybe Brian didn't need to freak out either. Life would work out. From the mouths of babes ...

Brian began a well-deserved time of personal reflection, thinking about what he wanted to do, about who he was and what he knew.

He challenged himself to clarify what he was bringing to the marketplace and how he could best market his most precious product: himself. He crafted his resume, tore it apart, and wrote it again. At his company-sponsored meetings with the outplacement firm, Brian began to learn many of the tips and techniques for finding a good job; he began to take some concrete steps into the future instead of worrying or waiting for the future to come to him.

He couldn't help but notice the anger of many of the people at the meetings. The stories poured out about the many years of service, the unrecognized loyalty, the years of sacrifice, and for what? *If only management had been doing what they were paid to do, to keep their eye on the future, to anticipate the industry changes. All of this could have been avoided. And the unions too. And the customers. Everyone had a role in this debacle. If only those idiots had done what they were supposed to do!*

Brian saw the world from a different view. Sure, there were times when the corporate decisions didn't make sense. Like when some of the good leaders, who had taken the company to success, had been let go in the early rounds of layoffs. But Brian's world was one of possibilities, a world of abundance with many opportunities. He would drift back to frustration from time to time, and even denial, waiting to wake up from this weird dream. But Brian came to an acceptance of his new existence and made the best of it.

There is a reality out there that none of us control. But we *always* have a choice in our response to it, no matter what life brings our way. Close to 70 percent of new jobs come from networking, and so for Brian it was a time to reach out to friends and colleagues from the past, together on a mission to support one another.

It was also a time that strengthened Brian's faith and his ability to, in turn, reach out and help others. It was an opportunity to do something different. He committed to enjoy the transition, no matter how scary it got, and to grow as much as possible. Starting over can be a once-in-a-lifetime chance to stretch out and try something new.

Not everyone copes with the vortex as well as my friend Brian. His attitude helped him to find another job in just a couple of months, despite fierce competition at the time.

I have coached many leaders through job loss and their subsequent transition. The reaction after finding a new job is always the same: *I wish that I had had faith in myself and enjoyed my time off!* If we do have trust that life will work out, one way or another, we can give ourselves permission to enjoy the journey so much more. Why not believe that life will work out and that you will be successful?

## Elisabeth Kübler-Ross

Even among the most optimistic, a major life change is a significant emotional event and a catalyst for some difficult times. We all experience misery.

In her landmark book, *On Death and Dying*, Elisabeth Kübler-Ross wrote the classic work on grief. She described five stages of grief that humans experience after a great loss:[24]

> 1.  **Denial**: *This can't be happening to me!* Headcount reduction is something that happens to other people that we read about in the media, but not to us. Employees often watch and worry as their organizations shrink but, in some way, never truly believe that it could happen to them. After all, we are all embedded with that sure formula for success that was drilled into us by our parents, teachers, and coaches early on: *If you are honest and work hard, you will be successful in life and move ahead. If you work hard enough, you will find a way to succeed.*
>
> When danger signs begin to appear on the horizon, when the market gets soft, when an organization begins to falter and feel budget constraints, people delude themselves. We suffer from the illusion of impending stability: *As soon as*

*things settle down around here, we can get back to normal!* All we have to do is work a little harder, just to catch up, and soon things will settle down.

And then one day comes that tap on the shoulder. The surprise and panic can be mind numbing. *This cannot be happening!* It is like a bad dream that one expects to wake from. Then we wake up the next morning, and the reality is still there. It is hard to believe that it could happen to us.

When someone finds out from his physician that he has terminal cancer, he wants a second opinion. *I have been eating well and exercising for years. How can this be? There must be some mistake.* When someone loses a job in a restructuring, or when she gets fired or retires, the common reaction is also disbelief. Somehow the final act in the play cannot be fair. It just doesn't seem possible. The walk to the parking lot and the drive away from work for the last time, they just don't seem real.

2.    **Anger**: After denial comes a second emotional response to loss: anger, often accompanied by blame. A typical early reaction is to look outside of ourselves for the cause of our misfortune, to look for the reason that we are no longer in control or happy. In a situation where one discovers that he has terminal cancer, anger and blame might be directed toward the doctor who made the diagnosis. A patient might believe that his doctor did not detect the problem while it was still curable. Maybe there is malpractice and maybe not, but humans tend to look for someone to blame. Maybe it is a tobacco company that through advertising encouraged us to smoke cigarettes. Maybe it is the restaurant that urged us to *supersize it*, to consume more than an ideal diet. *Someone is going to pay!*

When people are let go from a job, there can be lots of villains. Maybe there are true scoundrels, for example, when another employee or a manager has stolen company funds. Even when there are no obvious thieves or evil-doers, our reaction is to be angry with someone who we believe might have been able to do something to prevent our plight. Employees blame management for not steering the organization in another direction or anticipating a downturn. In turn managers blame employees for a lack of commitment and dedication. There are always lots of reasons to point fingers.

*Couldn't somebody have done something? Someone must be at fault!* We live in a litigious society that has learned to look for scoundrels. Good guys versus bad guys, heroes versus villains—that makes for a good movie storyline, but real work life is often much more complex. People like Bernie Madoff do steal other people's money, but nobody wants to restructure and reduce headcount for the fun of it. Headcount reduction is one of the most difficult actions a senior executive might be required to take throughout an entire career. Even if anger is justified, we need to get through and past it as soon as possible. Anger and blame never help us get what we really want: to move our lives on to the next phase in the journey.

**3. Bargaining**: People who learn that they have a terminal illness often find their way to religion. Some return years after losing their faith, and some come to religion for the first time. When life brings us to our knees, we find comfort in staying there. The plea is common: *Please God, give me just a little longer, and I promise that I will live a good life.*

At critical junctures in life, people commit to all of the things they have been meaning to get to—to be kinder to others, to be healthier, to work harder—to live a better life. People ask for divine intervention or human intervention from their employer, to give them one more chance to demonstrate their loyalty. During bargaining we plead for one more chance to get back what we are losing, to go back to the way things were. We will do almost anything for one more chance.

We pray to God to help us keep our jobs, and to our bosses to give us another opportunity. We offer to work more hours, whatever it takes, and maybe to stay on for less compensation. We go through this ritual even when, like my friend Brian, we know it is time to move on, to renew our professional growth, to come alive again. Even when our jobs are far from perfect, at least it is a way of life that we know, where we can continue to survive. An unknown future can be a very scary reality to face, whether we are moving on to the afterlife or to a life here on earth, without a clear purpose for getting up in the morning.

A common form of bargaining can occur even before someone experiences loss. When we see the writing on the wall, the signs that tell us that life is not working smoothly any longer, we often begin a bargaining phase. It happens when the workload slows down, or even when work gets extremely heavy for the thinned-out workforce left behind to do more with less. When we can see far enough down the road to know that the current life cycle will not last, we begin to bargain. We work harder, we work faster, we work longer hours—all in the hope of a reprieve. The implicit assumption is that if only we work a little more, we can avoid the inevitable.

Bargaining is about taking one last stand and hoping beyond hope that we can keep the old game going.

**4.** **Depression**: After a time of hoping against reality, we give up. Upon reaching depression we get tired of fighting the battle and resign ourselves to whatever comes our way. It can be a time of hopelessness and resignation, acknowledgment that our efforts are useless. Sometimes the depression phase is fleeting, and sometimes it lasts for a long time, signaling a need for professional support such as counseling or even pharmaceutical assistance.

The experience of depression can range from deep clinical depression to a temporary lull in the doldrums. Many see this time as a truly negative experience, a sign of life that has gone terribly wrong in a culture where success means being eternally optimistic. On the contrary, we get temporarily depressed for some very good reasons. It is a time when people shut down for a while, with a healthy benefit of getting recharged and building the strength to continue.

Depression has a valuable place in our survival as a human race. From time to time we need to catch our breath and take a moment to experience our emotional pain, not just to gloss over or suppress it. Depression is a time to heal. It can become a problem if it lasts for a long time and becomes a deep clinical depression, but it is simply part of the healing process.

Getting to depression is one of the reasons that the job of finding a new job is the toughest job of all. Maintaining the right energy to network, to write new letters, and to send out more resumes can be draining. It is very difficult for most people to maintain a constant search for eight to ten hours a day. On some days it all seems hopeless. Life never is, but it seems that way. We need to find the best way to stay energized and to put our best face forward. Sometimes a lull in the action is good.

The most important reason to understand that depression is natural and an expected part of grief is that it is normal. If you get depressed when you lose your job or a loved one or your health, *you are normal.* If you become convinced that it is time to give up, it really isn't, but you might just be depressed. It happens for a good reason.

People who lose their jobs begin to doubt themselves and to lose self-confidence. It is easy to believe that life will never be as good again. But we all thought that life would never be as good as our senior year in high school, and thank goodness we're not still back there. The high schools would begin to get crowded.

It is also typical for someone to believe that he or she will never be as good as in a past life stage. If you begin to believe that, it is absolutely not true. Think back to your previous life curve when you were at the top of your game, and remember all of the skills and value that you brought to work. Remember all of the strengths that got you to where you are, and simply accept the fact that you might be depressed. It's normal, and it's a good thing. You may not end up in life where you planned, but it is critical to know that it will be someplace good. Life always works out.

Anyone who stays depressed for a time needs to find someone to talk to. It can be a therapist, a professional coach, or maybe a physician. Maybe it can be a good friend or a partner. It is important not to suffer through it alone, and there are so many sources. Just reach out. There is always a hand waiting.

**5.** **Acceptance**: When we are lucky enough to get through depression, we often discover great peace of mind. At that point we know we have come to acceptance. Of course we might cycle back through all of the phases again the next day and even one hundred times again in the future, but it is important to get through to acceptance.

At acceptance we make peace with our reality. We accept our life for what it is and for what it will become. When Eugene O'Kelly accepted his inevitable death from incurable brain tumors in *Chasing Daylight*, he earned the privilege of enjoying every single moment of the rest of his life here on earth. From his perspective that was a rare blessing: to know he would die and yet to have the time to thank all of the people who made a difference in his life. Many never have that chance.

When we get to acceptance, we realize that our life *is what it is*. We can give up, or we can make it anything we want. Life often has unique twists and turns waiting for us that we never could have planned, and so it might not turn out like we had planned, but life is full of rich opportunities that are waiting ahead.

Acceptance is a great place to be, because we can focus energy on the things we need to do to move our lives ahead. If we receive a terminal diagnosis, we can plan our final arrangements and say our goodbyes, enjoying the time we have here on earth. If we lose a loved one, we can start living again, just the way our loved one would want us to. If we lose our health, we can be thankful for being alive and for what we have. If we lose a job, we can begin putting our full effort into the next step in our career and our journey.

There are ways of thinking about and framing our worlds that help us get to acceptance, but none of us is likely to just skip over the first four phases of grief, at least not for long. We are more likely destined to plod through each phase at least once. But that's okay because it is just part of being human and the way we are wired. Wherever we find ourselves, we can eventually get through.

Even when we understand the stages of grief and how to recognize them, there is no skipping the ride. Despite intellectual clarity, we still go through the grief.

If someone is clinically depressed, it is not enough to say, *You should just get on with your life. This is irrational, so just get over it.* Maybe grief doesn't appear to be rational, but we are still going to experience it.

People who are alive experience death in various forms. Those who have lost a child say that it is unlike any other grief. So losing a job is all relative, even though it may seem unbearable at times. Whatever the source, you cannot really know what grief is like until you experience loss.

You cannot skip stages and there is no strict timetable. Despite what any pundits might predict, people move through their grief journeys at their own pace. Multiple stages can come all at once. The intense pain of the early stages will not last, but the process takes time.

At some point you might feel a big hole in life that seems impossible to fill. But in time, if you want to, you get through it and move on with life.

## A Matter of Choice

Whether we accept or resist them, life's changes keep coming. Our success in navigating through change has a lot to do with the choices we make and how we think about it. The growth curve reminds us that life really is about an ongoing series of cycles. No matter what the leaders of our institutions do, no matter how smart and benevolent they are, we are destined to experience transformation.

The hidden blessing in having to reframe the world around us and who we are in it is that we are required to grow. While we might not prefer to experience deep loss and to wade through the stages of grief, we are going to anyway. We might as well learn as much as we can on the voyage and become stronger in the process. The speed at which we find our way to acceptance, and the quality of the journey, depends on our perspective.

In other words we don't always choose the events that occur in our lives, but we always choose how we look at life. The Choice Cycle tells a simple story about the role of our thinking and the choices we make.[25]

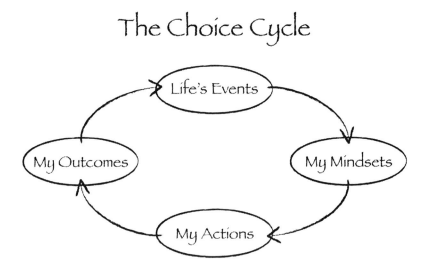

**The Choice Cycle**

The outcomes that we create in our lives depend upon our actions, which are driven by our mindsets, or how we think about the world around us. While we only influence the outcomes we create and we certainly don't control what happens to us (our life events), we *always* choose how we think and feel about life.

When life requires us to start over, when we have lost something important and we need to reinvent ourselves, we need to find our way to acceptance. After we have trudged through all of the phases of grief and back again, we are still left with a basic choice. At a fundamental level we need to decide how we view the change we are going through: Is our world falling apart, or is our life recombining to something better? Are we going through entropy or syntropy? Life doesn't really decide that question for us. We do.

> "We don't receive wisdom,
> we must discover it for ourselves,
> after a journey
> that no one can take for us or spare us."
> —Marcel Proust

# 8

## Future Focus

> "We shall not cease from exploration,
> and the end of all our exploring
> will be to arrive where we started
> and know the place for the first time."
>
> —T. S. Eliot

### Tino Wallenda

I have often considered the plight of young Tino Wallenda. Now let me say right up front that I'm not sure if any of the Wallenda children have actually thought about their heritage this way. But I can imagine the pit in his stomach when Tino, at around six years old, reached the age of reason. He must have suddenly realized that he had been born into the most famous aerialist, tightrope-walking family in the world, The Flying Wallendas.

Holy moly! Can you imagine the day his famous grandfather, Karl, asked Tino if he wanted to work in the family business? Supposedly children don't actually choose the families they are born into, but I can imagine that more than one of the Wallenda offspring wondered if life was really all that fair.

Tino, of course, shared Karl's genes for adventure and jumped at the chance. If any of the Wallenda kids ran away from home, they must have wanted to run away *from* the circus, not with the circus.

The Wallendas began their tradition back in 1780 when they became a family circus act, traveling through the villages of Europe demonstrating their talents as acrobats, jugglers, clowns, animal trainers, and trapeze artists. In the 1800s they became best known for their skill and daring on the flying trapeze.

**The Wallendas circa 1900**

Karl Wallenda, the patriarch of the modern-day Wallenda family, was born in Magdeburg, Germany, in 1905. He began performing with the family at age six and training on the high wire at around age fifteen, during the Great Depression. Karl was an experienced tightrope walker by his late teens and at the age of twenty, began his own act, recruiting his brother Herman and a friend named Josef Geiger. In 1927 they added a young teenage girl, Helen Kreis, who later became Karl's wife.

With Karl in the lead, the Wallendas were contracted by John Ringling and became a lead act in the Ringling Brothers, Barnum & Bailey Circus, the "Greatest Show on Earth." In 1928, they introduced their act to fans at Madison Square Garden, performing without a net, because it had been lost in transit. Not using a net became their trademark, holding their audiences breathless, as they performed their death-defying show. Today they never even practice with a net and consider it a false security.

While performing their act for a crowd in Akron, Ohio, in the 1940s, four members fell all at once, but stayed on the wire. None was seriously hurt, and the next day a reporter stated that they had fallen so gracefully that it seemed as if they were flying. The headlines of the article read "The Flying Wallendas," and the name stuck.

Karl went on to form his own circus while developing hair-raising acts, including their most famous, The Seven. The stunt was a seven-person formation in which seven members of the group created a three-level structure, using a chair at the top. Connected together in a pyramid formation, they traversed the tightrope together, thirty-five feet above the ground.

The feat worked perfectly for fourteen years until January 30, 1962, when the troupe fell in Detroit. Three men fell to the ground, two of whom died that night. The third was Mario Wallenda, who survived but was paralyzed from the waist down. In a tribute to those who died, The Seven was performed only twice in the next thirty-five years: one year later in 1963 and then again in 1977. The Seven was reintroduced in 1998 and is still performed today.

Karl continued performing with a smaller group and graduated to Sky Walks—walking on tightropes strung between buildings, across stadiums, and over canyons. In 1978, Karl fell to his death, at the age of seventy-three, while performing in San Juan, Puerto Rico. He was reported to have fallen because of high winds, but the cause was later determined to be faulty guy wires strung along the tightrope cable. Karl did not fall because of his age or physical ability. His legacy lives on in the proud Wallenda family and their many troupes who still perform today.

Karl's wife, Helen, was interviewed by Warren Bennis in 1985 in a study that led to a book, coauthored with Burt Nanus, entitled *Leaders: The Strategies for Taking Charge.*[26] Karl's life was used to illustrate a characteristic of great leaders that Bennis and Nanus described as "a way of responding to failure as a learning experience." Karl Wallenda put his focus and total energy into his work and thought of his "failures," like the fall in Detroit, as life experiences from which he could learn and grow.

Karl saw each of his failures as a new beginning, not as an end. Karl died, but we are all going to die, and Karl died reaching for life, not avoiding death.

If Karl Wallenda can get back on the tightrope, what is the lesson for any of us who are required by life to start over? When we get depressed and want to give up, is there an inner reservoir of strength and courage that we can call upon? It was Karl's transformative leadership style that inspired his family and their colleagues to become the best in the world at their craft.

Karl was one of the first Wallenda children to be brought into the family act, but not the last. The Wallenda family extended on to seven generations through his grandchildren and great-grandchildren. Many of them continue in the family business today, performing for the Shrine Circus.

But back to the story of Tino Wallenda. What did Karl teach Tino, his grandson and protégé, when Tino started in the family business? Karl invited Tino into the troupe when he was only seven years old by taking him into the backyard and putting a balance pole in his hands. Karl taught him how to place his feet, how to control his body, and where to focus his eyes. At the age of twelve, Tino made his first crossing of a wire that was thirty-five feet in the air. By seventeen, Tino was a full-fledged member of the Flying Wallendas.

Don't you wonder what Karl Wallenda and the other Wallenda elders learned about helping youngsters to discover their courage and about facing extremely difficult life challenges?

**Alex Wallenda, Karl's great-grandson
making his debut on the high wire**

What could they teach someone who faces the daunting challenge of reinventing his or her life? Think about their skill in coaxing a young family member to walk across a cable that is thirty-five feet in the air.

As I was growing up, working in the family garden seemed like hard work. We weren't the Wallendas, but my family story makes me wonder about them. How was the Wallenda family consistently able to incorporate the next generation into the act?

My theory has always been that beyond the many practical skills involved in walking across a tightrope (or working a family garden, for that matter), there were three essential elements to making Tino successful (and I thank my colleague and friend Patrick Edwards for sharing the story of Tino Wallenda):

1.      **A compelling vision**: I can just imagine Tino, standing on a small platform, maybe only ten or twelve feet off the ground, getting ready to make his first walk across the tightrope cable. Tino would have needed a compelling vision to get started.

One of the first things that Karl Wallenda would have needed to do is to get Tino to focus on the other platform, his destination. It was not just to the other platform, of course, but to the future success that the other platform symbolized. Getting to the other platform would mean a huge step forward, acceptance into a proud family heritage, a chance to prove his worth to the Wallenda family, in a sense, a passage into adulthood.

The vision would have to be a *compelling* vision—an image that pulled Tino into his future. That vision would have to be strong enough to get a young man to take physical risk at a time in his life when he did not yet have the self-confidence and the courage of the family elders. Unstable steps and unsure psyche—the future possibilities would have to pull at Tino's mind and heart strongly enough to overcome all of his fear. For Tino to be successful, he must have wanted to get to that other platform in a serious way.

**2.     Letting go**: Karl knew that if he could get Tino to the other platform for the first time, Tino would be making a step change into his future. He also knew from experience that the journey across started with a first step. And to take that first step, Tino would have needed to let go of the platform that he was clinging to.

A first step into any new future means letting go of whatever you are attached to that keeps you in place. My guess is Tino was steadying himself on the platform with every ounce of energy he had. After years of conducting high-ropes courses in the adventure learning field, I know what it means to *hug a pole for dear life*. Been there, done that. That platform would have represented something solid to hang onto and all of the security in the world. It must have been comforting for Tino just to stay there, just to hold on, just for one more minute.

Karl would have known that the first step in a journey forward means letting go of that sanctuary. A new security would have to spring from the confidence that comes from success. *Let go, Tino. Take just one step forward!*

**3.     Support**: What if you were in little Tino's shoes? What would you need to get you to take that first step into the future? Most of us would need someone underneath, in case we don't make it across on the first try. There would be plenty of days in the future to work up to thirty-five feet and no net underneath—the Wallenda family's trademark. As we start something brand new, the willingness to take the risk would come from the knowledge that if we fell, there would be someone to catch us.

People are willing to take lots of risk and to try lots of new things if they believe they will be safe doing it. That is the power of support. In the Western culture, we tend to be rugged individualists, especially in the United States. We like to believe that we are strong enough to do it all alone, and that asking for support is a sign of weakness. For people who are making a big life change, however, support can mean the difference between getting locked in place, doing the same things day after day, or reaching out to find something new. Karl Wallenda would have known this principle from firsthand experience.

Think for a moment about the wisdom of a natural leader like Karl Wallenda. If you find yourself in a place where you need to start over, to take a step change into your future, are all three essential elements in place? A compelling vision, the ability to let go, and support?

Have you discovered a vision for the future that is so strong that it will compel you to move forward? In other words, could you imagine a future that would pull you through all of the hard work and risk?

Is there something you are holding on to or attached to that is keeping you in place, something you need to let go of? Are you trying to drive ahead but with the parking brake on? Maybe it is a notion of who you used to be or of who you thought you were. Perhaps it is doubt that you can be successful, or that you can find true happiness. Maybe it means simply forgiving someone else, or even forgiving yourself.

And finally do you have a support network in place to take a big step out there? If you are reinventing yourself, maybe you can't do it all alone.

Starting over in life often means a step change. For some it means leaving one job and getting another just like it down the street. For many it is more than that and requires a beginner's mind—rethinking who you are and who you want to be. A compelling vision, letting go, and support—all are critical ingredients in the formula for moving forward.

A first step includes deciding on a positive vision for the future. It's important to take some time to reflect not only on your life purpose and who you are at the core but also on where you will be in the future. It's a timeless formula for success: decide on where you want to go, and if you do, you will be much more likely to get there. It is a simple formula, but not always easy to do. That is why taking time to reflect is so critical.

Starting over can be a lot of very hard work. As human beings we are able to cope with all kinds of flak along the way if we have a strong and clear vision that pulls us through and helps us transcend the challenges.

What is a future that would get you up in the morning to do whatever it takes?

## The Law of Attraction

The best-selling book and video *The Secret* reminded us all of the power inherent in a vision focused on the results we want out of life.[27,28] The message is known as "The Law of Attraction"—we attract the things into our lives that we truly focus on. Life provides our most desirable outcomes if we can create a strong enough vision.

The Law of Attraction doesn't mean that we can simply wish for a new Cadillac and one will appear in the driveway, or that we can clap our hands and be instantly cured of cancer. The Law of Attraction is validated by the evidence of vision and focus in those who drive toward success.

The core lesson in the Law of Attraction is that if we spend our precious life energy focused on the outcomes we want, we are more likely to get them. If we focus on the things we *do not want*, or worry about what could go wrong, we are not focusing on *what we want* and are likely to be less successful.

If we spend time wondering if something bad will happen, or focus on the circumstances in our lives that we don't like, those are the things we are likely to get. What we resist, persists.

If focusing on the results we want is like praying for success, worrying is like praying for failure. In other words, if we waste energy whining about what we don't like in life, that is what we are likely to get. We are simply wasting precious energy that could be used constructively.

It's not really all that complex. People who get what they want out of life focus their energy on positive outcomes. Others who can't seem to discover their dreams get attached to their fears and worries.

Can you think of a time in your life when you really wanted something and, through dedication and effort, made that dream into a reality? Most successful people have several stories where that principle plays out in their lives. Sincere intention must be coupled with action. As Ben Franklin mused, "God helps those who help themselves." In any case, accomplishment begins with clear purpose and intent.

In 1983, my wife, Shirley, and I decided to adopt children. Shirley was adopted herself, and adoption was something we genuinely wanted from life. In those early days of independent adoption, we met a supportive attorney who convinced us that if we were truly dedicated, we could make it happen.

We created a personal flyer with our picture and a poem, as well as our request to the universe for support in our mission. We mailed the flyer to hundreds of doctors whose addresses I copied from hotel room phone books found in my travels throughout the United States. This all happened before popular use of the Internet. We told everyone we talked to about our goal. We prayed and we pleaded—it had become almost an obsession for us. We were determined to be successful.

A couple of months after we started our search, a client with a tight budget asked me to do some work at a discounted fee. They were a major airline and added the stipulation that if I were willing to work for less, they would pay for Shirley's flights and other expenses as well so she could come along with me. There would be two engagements, and the opportunity created a couple of welcome mini-vacations for us. We scheduled the work and flights weeks ahead of time.

Just before it was time for us to leave for the first trip, we received a call from a physician in the same city we were traveling to. The doctor had arranged for an interview with an expectant mother—

something we were able to do on the days we planned to be in town. You can guess the rest of the story. The interview went great, and the expectant mother gave birth to our first son, Bill, exactly on the dates of my second client project.

When we asked the birth mother if she had considered any names for her new child, she mentioned "William David." Shirley and I sat in awe. That was the same name we had planned if the baby was a boy. William David is my name too. I wanted to name my son after me, just as my father had, and his father before him.

Only three and one-half months passed from the day that we committed to adopt children to the day that we were flying home together, in first class on a flight paid for by my client, with a new infant son. Independent adoption is surely not as easy today as it was, but we adopted four children in two and one-half years. The contacts we made allowed us to help one other couple find an infant to adopt too.

We were blessed and lucky, but the incredible circumstances were too apparent to ignore. There was too much evidence not to believe in the power of a clear vision and of expressing one's intent to the universe. We took a lot of actions that helped that vision become a reality, but it all begins with a clear commitment and a vision. It was the Law of Attraction at work.

Let me be clear and practical. If you are looking for a new job or searching for the next stage in your life's journey, it may not be sufficient to express your intention to the universe. Don't expect God to whisper in the ear of a prospective employer, to send them looking for you or calling your house in search of someone with exactly your talents.

This is true no matter how devout your prayers. God can give you the strength to get through the transition, but He probably won't send a job to your doorstep. Sitting around and wishing will lead to disappointment.

By the same accord, if you create a clear vision for success and are willing to act, your actions will automatically and perhaps even subconsciously lead you to that vision.

If you become attached to fear, to visions of failure, to worry about the future, to believing your task is impossible, the world is very capable of serving up those outcomes too. If your spirit reflects your fear of the negative possibilities, you won't reflect your best energy. If you go to interviews desperate, that mood will come across in subtle ways you won't be able to hide.

So decide what you want to create and focus all of your energy on it!

A powerful aspect of a clear vision is the strength we acquire to get through difficult times. Much like Tino Wallenda, we need a platform at the far end of the tightrope to focus on to make our journey there less treacherous and fearful. If our vision is strong, our focus is out on the horizon, looking to where we are going.

If our vision is weak, we focus on the immediate moment and all of the challenges and obstacles that wear us down. We can eventually convince ourselves that our effort is useless and that the world is hopeless.

The principle is simple: imagining a future so compelling and enjoyable that you would be willing to endure extreme hardship in the hope of achievement. This is the very rule that gets a gifted craftsman through a difficult apprenticeship, a medical student through thirty-six-hour work shifts as an intern, or an athlete through a triathlon.

Vision gets a soldier through battle and back home safe. Alternatively, it allows one to sacrifice his life for a cause. If a future scenario is forceful enough, anything is possible.

For those in life starting over and fighting the daily battle to find new footing, a picture of a new and exciting future is invaluable. Finding that vision or new purpose is a challenge, but it lies in focusing on an ideal future, not in ruminating over a pile of problems.

Our inner wisdom can lead us to that purpose if we listen. What have we done that leads us to joy? What are our true strengths? What were we born to do? To learn?

Perhaps we are all born with a code that shows us the way, in any circumstance, and part of our life's journey is to decipher it. Maybe the code is embedded within us, somehow, and we are born with the wisdom and knowledge to find our path, no matter what.

Whether we are born with a purpose and embedded archetypes, or we simply gravitate to our purpose through experience, it is out there waiting for each of us, to be discovered. The best place to start is right here, right where you are, and the best time is right now.

"Life is being on the wire; everything else is waiting."

—Karl Wallenda

# 9

## Play to Win

"Whoever can see through all fear will always be safe."

—Tao Te Ching

### The End of the World

You may have heard the adage, "When others around me are losing their jobs, it means we are in a recession. When I lose my job, it means that we are in a depression."

Recent world developments have many leaning toward the depression scenario. The cataclysmic economic events that had been brewing for years but fully emerged in 2008 were shocking in both their global scope and depth. In most of our lifetimes, they were unprecedented.

The financial crisis that started on Wall Street and touched every one of us on Main Street brought some giants to their knees. Who would have ever guessed that it was possible for Lehman Brothers to claim bankruptcy? Wasn't Merrill Lynch the very symbol of a bullish world, bent on growth and expansion? As General Motors goes, so goes the economy. Is it possible that General Motors and Chrysler both filed for bankruptcy, and in the same year? How could all of this have happened in a post-1930s, Great Depression America, where we had already learned from our history?

Treasury Secretary Timothy Geithner testified in June 2009 before the Senate Banking Committee that our economy hit a wall in the United States, at least in part, because of a collapse in the derivatives markets. Derivatives are financial instruments whose value is "derived" from something else, such as a mortgage-backed security. What?

Warren Buffett later described derivatives as "investments of mass destruction," a play on words that reflected his own losses. They are basically *side bets* on the performance of other investments, a form of gambling that was made illegal in the United States after the 1929 market crash. The average individual investor probably doesn't know what a derivative is, much less how to invest in one.

We can only conclude that despite the "just stick with it" formula espoused by our parents that hard work doesn't always lead to success. In reality, forces that are way beyond our control can make a big impact on our livelihoods.

When we lose our means of livelihood, it can seem as if the whole world is crumbling around us. Does it ever seem to you like the world is coming to an end? Many people actually think so. Maybe it is, maybe it isn't. How do you know?

A growing number of observers see the signs in ancient prophecies by famous individuals like Michel de Nostredame, better known to us as Nostradamus.

While there are always diverse interpretations of world trends, some look to the Book of Revelation in the Bible, observing the natural disasters and other catastrophes that they claim are evidence of an apocalypse, the judgment of God.

Others point to the end of the Mayan calendar and its 5,126-year era, which occurs on the winter solstice, December 21, 2012. As evidence that doomsday thinking has hit the mainstream, *USA Today* published an article on March 27, 2007, that describes the emergence of fears about the 2012 prediction.[29] In the article headlined "Does Maya Calendar Predict 2012 Apocalypse?" author G. Jeffrey MacDonald effectively summarizes the diverse points of view currently espoused in the many topical books published in recent years.

A good deal of interest was piqued in director Mel Gibson's 2006 film about the Mayan civilization, *Apocalypto*. Some authors are forecasting a variety of environmental catastrophes while others predict a more positive result, a fundamental shift in human consciousness.

The Mayas were a pre-Columbian civilization that reached their peak from 300 to 900 A.D. They lived on the Yucatan Peninsula, in current day Mexico, and in Guatemala and Belize. The Mayas were especially advanced in their knowledge of architecture (including pyramids), hieroglyphic writing, and mathematics. They used the number "zero" in their calculations, something the Romans had not yet done. While they had a truly advanced culture for their time, the Mayas were also big on human sacrifice, vividly portrayed in *Apocalypto*. I suppose that *advanced* is a relative term.

The Mayas disappeared as a nation after 900, and nobody is exactly sure why. Proposed theories include widespread crop disease to pestilence brought by the Spanish conquistadors who marched in with minor resistance. In history's view, an advanced society was gone in the blink of an eye, but they left a legacy in their 5,126-year calendar.

The Mayan calendar was developed after years of studying the constellations, but then officially ignored when the Spanish brought their Gregorian calendar, the one most popular today. Many who study the measurement of time marvel at the accuracy of the Mayan schedule. Despite its ancient origins, it doesn't need regular adjustments like the Gregorian calendar, which uses "leap years" to get back on track.

On December 21, 2012, at 11:11 Universal Time, the current cycle will be complete. What does all of this mean? Some say global catastrophe, while others proclaim a worldwide spiritual awakening and a change in the nature of consciousness. Several writers are predicting ecological disasters, as the earth's sun becomes aligned with the Milky Way Galaxy for the first time in twenty-six thousand years. Others even predict a reversal of the earth's axes. Holy moly, if I wake up in China the next morning, I am going to be really confused.

A few serious scholars deride the doomsayers as charlatans who are trying to cash in on public fears. In reality, none of us really knows what will happen, simply because we haven't been there yet. Nobody knows what will happen when the sun is aligned with the center of the Milky Way for the first time in twenty-six thousand years. None of us was around the last time it happened, and so who would know?

My bet is on the *change in consciousness* theory, as we grow and learn as human beings. But are the Mayan calendar and 2012 connected in any way? And are we headed to a higher plane of thinking or a growing polarization of values? Will the change require a revolutionary and possibly painful transition via an apocalyptic event? Or will the veil be removed from our eyes in a transcendental wave of enlightenment?

One conclusion is that it really doesn't matter. We need to prepare ourselves for whatever comes our way, no matter what it is. Maybe the world will end when the caldera buried beneath Yellowstone National Park erupts, or maybe a giant asteroid will collide with the earth. Perhaps a roaming black hole will swallow our solar system, or a flu pandemic will wipe us off the earth. Maybe the dinosaurs will come back to life and eat us! It really doesn't matter.

The end of the world, at least as we know it, could be at our doorstep. Whatever happens, it is clear that, like the derivatives markets, it is way beyond our control. What is in our control is the choice we each will make every day about how we live our lives. Whether we are waiting in anticipation of December 21, 2012, or for the apocalypse, or for a healthier economy, we can always choose. We can always choose how we think about the world around us and how we react, no matter what happens.

There are always a long list of reasons why success is doubtful, if not impossible, in any life venture. There is an equally long list of reasons why success in life is *possible*. Success has a lot to do with the list of reasons we choose to believe. Why do some people take huge steps in life, while others observe and give credence to the obstacles? Even when the playing field and life circumstances are not the same, resourceful people find a way to move on.

**Play to Win or Play Not to Lose?**

As mentioned earlier in Chapter 5, when any one of us hits a wall, or sees a possible wall coming in our path, we make a choice: Am I going to play to win or play not to lose? Am I going to go all out to make the best of life given the circumstances and create the best possible outcomes given the resources I have? Or I am going to go into survival mode, to hunker down and play it safe, to avoid risk and be cautious? In a fundamental way, the question is this: Am I going to focus on what I want to create and make my best effort, or am I going to focus on the things I do not want and use my energy to avoid what I fear?

If everything does change on December 21, 2012, I want to be moving forward, not using all of my time and resources digging a bunker. If it does get that bad, sayonara my friends. It's not a bad idea to have some emergency rations in the basement in case of a natural disaster, but I will never center my life around preparing to avoid one.

Jim Jackson, a gifted public speaker who is known as The Harley Guy, describes the "Harley Attitude" as "Going as hard as you can, with all you can, as far as you can!" That is playing to win. The words *playing to win* or *playing not to lose* can make the concept seem trite, but at a basic level it is about your mindset and values for life. If we are going to survive and thrive when we are starting over, the best we get out of playing not to lose is staying safe. Chances are we will not reach our potential by holding back.

What exactly are we afraid of? In their book, *Play to Win! Choosing Growth over Fear in Work and Life*, Larry and Hersch Wilson described their concept of the four fatal fears:[30]

1. **I fear failure—I need to succeed.** Another way to talk about a fear of failure is all about a strong desire to win, or to always be in control. In our highly competitive culture, winning gets twisted into being better than someone else. A mindset of playing to win defines winning as being the best you can be, given your own ability, not compared to someone else.

2. **I fear being wrong—I need to be right.** A slightly different way to think about a fear of being wrong is the drive to save face, to look good to others at all times, not as someone who could or would make a mistake. It is about our tendency to project a façade to others that communicates that we are in control, that we know what we are doing, and that we could not be wrong.

3. **I fear rejection—I need to be accepted.** Fear of rejection is about a need for approval and acceptance from others. We have all experienced it walking across that dance floor as freshmen in high school, standing up to make a speech in front of our peers, or completing that application for our first job. It is about a desire to be loved and accepted.

4. **I fear being emotionally uncomfortable—I need to be comfortable.** Fear of emotional discomfort comes in a variety of forms and phobias, based on what makes each of us emotionally comfortable or, alternatively, out of whack.

We experience a fear of being emotionally uncomfortable when we have to sit down with someone to have a difficult conversation, maybe to resolve a conflict. Perhaps this fear hits us when we fall in front of our friends on an icy sidewalk. It's not so much the bump on the rear that hurts as much as our egos and our pride.

As Larry and Hersch Wilson point out, one strength of these fears is an assumption that we "need" some of these conditions to succeed, to be right, and so forth. Through our self-talk we suggest that these conditions are critical for achieving happiness when, in fact, many find ways to forgo these "needs" every day. I fail to succeed regularly. I am wrong more times than I would like to admit. Some people don't like me, and life is full of discomfort. If I convince myself that I need these conditions in my life, I am destined for fear. What we really *need* is air, food, water, shelter, and protection from the elements.

Whether these are real fears or simply perceived, they act on us in the same way. If any of these fears becomes dominant in our life, they become "fatal"—they inhibit growth and new life and bring us to a standstill in our learning. Our life purpose can lean toward staying safe, avoiding or escaping our fears, and not approaching the things we really want out of life. The best we get is not to lose, not to look bad, not to be uncomfortable. Life today simply doesn't permit us to be fearful and successful at the same time.

Do you see an emotional specialty of yours in the four fatal fears? Do one or two of these tug at you? If so, first of all, you are human. Yea! That's a good thing. But more importantly, maybe this is the window to your future personal growth and development, the kind of difficult and yet important inner work that can lead to a whole new level of satisfaction in this challenge we call life.

One purpose of the human mind is protection and survival. Human beings constantly scan the horizon for dangers and risks. We get this tendency honestly, from our ancestors, who made it through a physically challenging existence. While most of the risks in today's world are psychological instead of physical, we have adopted some unconscious habits that we employ to get through our lives.

Those traits are not all bad! But when fear becomes a dominant companion, when playing not to lose becomes a fundamental orientation to existence, we miss out on so much of life. And we stop learning and growing.

Letting go of fear entirely is probably not a wise strategy, or even possible, at least not without the use of mind-altering drugs that would surely cause other serious problems. Playing to win is not only about letting go of life-crimping fears, it is about building courage. Courage means acting in healthy ways despite fear, not by eliminating fear.

## Compete Against Yourself

John Wooden got it. The famous men's basketball coach from UCLA used playing to win as the philosophical foundation that led his teams to an unmatched ten national championships. Wooden had a lot of good players to help him execute his philosophy, but one big difference was his approach to his players.

Wooden defined his goal precisely: "Success is ... knowing you made the effort to become the best of which you are capable." He learned his secret of success from his father, Joshua Hugh Wooden, who told his son, "Don't worry about whether you're better than somebody else, but never cease trying to be the best you can become. You have control over that; the other you don't."[31]

John Wooden goes on to reinforce his message: "To my way of thinking, when you give your total effort—everything you have—the score can never make you a loser. And when you do less, it can't somehow magically turn you into a winner."

It would be easy for a skeptic or a cynic to claim that it is easy for the final score not to matter to someone who has won ten national championships and built a sports dynasty as well as anyone before or since. But Wooden understands that the path to a higher score, no matter the scorecard, is about using your resources to their full potential. The score and the championships are the outcome, the by-product of playing to win.

The journey is all about being the best that you can become. It is all you can do, really. It is the only true choice you have. The results will take care of themselves. Sometimes we win, and sometimes we don't, but anyone can be a winner if he or she puts in a full effort.

Wooden goes on to say: "Compete only against yourself. Remember my father's advice. Set your standards high; namely, do the absolute best of which you are capable. Focus on running the race rather than winning it. Do those things necessary to bring forth your personal best and don't lose sleep worrying about the competition. Let the competition lose sleep worrying about you."

Starting over in your career and in your life can be a very difficult time—a time of fear focused on survival instead of success. And yet it is a critical time in life to play to win—to act with courage and to go all out for the best possible outcome. When the formula for success that got you here will not be the formula that gets you there, life demands trying new things and getting comfortable being uncomfortable. Survival is not enough. Be the best you can be, and go for the best that you can become.

"You are not stuck where you are unless you decide to be."

—Wayne Dyer

# 10

## Practical Steps on a Path Forward

"When patterns are broken, new worlds emerge."

—Tuli Kupferburg

### Reaching Out

A majority of the message in this book is about creating the emotional muscle to live through difficult transition. The changes that life serves up can be very hard to get through, and so much of today's available guidance speaks only to the *tasks* in a job search. The human experience in pursuing that task, on the other hand, can be harder to manage.

Many excellent outplacement firms that specialize in helping displaced employees do a great job of teaching clients how to write better resumes, network, and interview well. Finding support in managing the human side of life change is less common. People typically suppress fear, try to project a good face, and participate in our cultural collusion: *Let's all pretend that everything is just fine!*

We create a façade for the public that communicates that we are strong and that we just have to keep a stiff upper lip and get on with it. The human side of the life change equation is often ignored, simply because it is hard to discuss.

Like a physician with poor bedside manners, it can be easier to talk about facts and data than underlying human emotion.

Hopefully some of the reflections here make your voyage through the vortex a little easier. With consciousness of the challenge, the conversation can be made public, out in the light. Maybe we can all share a little more compassion for anyone who faces the obstacles in starting life over.

My new personal hobby is having support meetings with clients who have become unemployed, typically not at their own choosing, to help them renew their careers. At first this free service seemed like a good marketing technique. The plan was that clients would find new jobs, and, in return for my kindness, they would hire me to work as their coach in the new organizations. In reality, this approach has never worked that well to get new business, but in the meantime, something special happened.

I found myself becoming attached to helping others, not to get anything back, but just because it was such a rewarding experience. Sustaining others became my way of doing something good for people who had supported me in the past and, in a bigger sense, my unique way of giving something back in a world that had blessed me with so much.

My hobby became a mission that I began to understand over time, as I learned from one job seeker and passed ideas to the next. I have been able to share best practices and to some extent simply provide much needed encouragement, to offer a push, and to remind my clients how good they are, both as performers and people. I remind them that *everyone* they know has found something as good as what they left, and if they will simply trust, life will work out for them too, and they will enjoy their search much more.

There are a lot of lessons learned. One valuable takeaway is that there are always next steps and that a career is never finished unless someone is ready to be finished. There is always a path forward for those who search with earnest. Another is once again that the journey always ends okay. Many don't find exactly what they want, or find that their search takes them on a far different path than they would ever have imagined, as life teaches us that our plans don't always count in the bigger scheme of things.

But everyone finds a way he or she can be happy. In really hard times some settle for less than what they want, as some jobs vanish and don't come back. But everyone finds something really good out there even if it takes longer than expected. Life works out.

Of course one lesson learned is the power of service to others. Reaching out a hand to help those who will in turn reach out to others, a pay-it-forward approach, is a powerful thing to observe. Collaboration and competition are both contagious, and we each make a choice. Whether there is a reward at the end of the rainbow or not, there is true joy is helping others today. Having a bad day? Help someone else in his or her life journey, and your day always gets better. Once again Gandhi's message comes to light: "Find yourself by losing yourself in the service of others." Boy, he was right. It all comes back.

Another reflection is that there is a real practical side to the work of starting over. The job of finding a new job may be the most difficult job of all, but several common sense practices can lead to success. In the next few pages are some that could be useful for you, that you can pick and choose from. They are a collection of techniques gathered over the years from people I have coached who have found new opportunities. They are proven.

There may not be any way to start over, to find a new position or career, without personal challenge. Everyone who accepts my guidance has struggled to let go of self-doubt, to maintain hope and optimism, and to remember all of the strengths that led to past life success. But overwhelmingly, the individuals I know have found better opportunities than the roles they left behind.

Some of the following approaches have led to better futures for a lot of job seekers. Do what works for you.

## Networking

According to the U.S. Bureau of Labor Statistics, 70 percent of all jobs are found through networking. Networking is not new news, for sure, but the way you approach building and using relationships in a search is important to success. Introductions to prospective employers that come from well-respected and influential people can make all the difference. The world of work has always been influenced by relationships. It is the grease that keeps the globe going around. So how do you come in contact with influential people?

Start with the people you know. One approach is to begin by making a long list of all of the people that you have come into contact with in your life. While older relationships may not be fresh, it is worthwhile to consider them potential resources in helping you move ahead with your life.

You never know—a long-lost friend might still be carrying some baggage or anger about something you said in college and not have the time of day for you. On the other hand, he might be *delighted* to hear from you again, and he might have learned just the day before about a position that would match your talents. More recent colleagues who know your current strengths are always better, but don't overlook an opportunity.

A primary reason people hesitate to network thoroughly is ego. We would like our friends and associates from the past to believe that we have been successful. Maintaining that image means that we may not want others to know that we need their help and support. If we define ourselves by our past titles—"I am a Vice President at Merrill Lynch."—it is difficult to maintain that façade when we are out of work. The last thing we might be inclined to do is to call everyone to announce it.

But announcing it to the whole world is exactly what you need to do. A committed networker lets everyone in the universe know, "Can you support me? I am in a search for the next step in my journey."

When we let the whole universe know what we want, the support that flows back is amazing.

So let go of your ego and realize that your success is never defined by a past, temporary position (they are all temporary) or a role you have played, but it is about you at your core. Your real success is about you as a person, your values, your strengths, your leadership capabilities, your interpersonal skills, your relationships, your commitment, and so forth. It is about you, not your job, so let the façade go.

Make that long contact list. The worst that can happen is that someone can hang up on you, but then you really won't have lost anything anyway. The relationship was already not healthy. Nobody ever died from this kind or rejection.

You might be surprised at what you discover, including the number of people who would genuinely like to help you. Probably a lot of the people you know have been in the same position and remember the appreciation of someone who gave some support. Good people want to help.

My suggestion is typically to make that list using software that allows you to work the list, for example, to capture contact information, to sort, to prioritize them, to schedule regular contacts, to record notes from your conversations, to schedule a follow-up contact, and so forth. Contact management software like Act! or Microsoft Office Outlook, or Microsoft Excel can be helpful tools.

Think back through your succession of life experiences and remember all of the people that you have worked with, whether in intact work teams or on special projects, and get them on your list. Think of people from organizations where you have worked, but also consider those outside of your work experience, such as people from your church or from civic committees. Maybe you know others with whom you have worked on community service projects, who have seen the very best side of you. List your personal friends too. Get them all on your list.

You might also prioritize or code your list based on your perception of each person's ability to help you find what you are looking for—maybe A's, B's, and C's. That coding should be flexible, as job seekers are constantly surprised by where valuable support comes from, and a C can quickly become an A.

Next, begin to work the list. E-mail or even texting can be useful in finding a time to schedule a conversation, but while electronic correspondence is safe and quick, it usually won't get you what you really want. Phone calls and, when possible, face-to-face conversations always seem to be more influential in getting others to actively support your search.

If you are going to use e-mail, send personal notes to individuals. While it is efficient to send the same note to a distribution list, many recipients will assume someone else will respond and help you. You become too easy to put off. If you send personalized e-mails to one person at a time, each individual is more likely to respond.

When others see your eyes or at least hear your voice, they are much more likely to take some action than they would otherwise to personally recommend you for a position. Given today's commonly accepted norms for ignoring and deleting e-mails in busy times, you become too easy to put off until later, and maybe until never.

Same thing for social networking Web sites. It is great to stay connected online and to have a Web site to send prospective employers to. That says something about your technology acumen. But don't rely on employers seeking and finding you, no matter how articulate your description of your abilities and experience.

A networking site is just that—a way to stay connected so that, when a conversation is of value, you are in touch and can make a request for a meeting. It is a location to connect. Get in front of people and let them know what you are looking for, and especially how they can help.

Before you have a networking meeting or phone conversation, do some planning to think about what you want to say and what support you will ask for. Don't assume your contacts will automatically know what you want from them and offer to help you. They certainly haven't thought about your situation as much as you have, so help them out by being straightforward.

Again, those of us who practice negative self-talk from time to time (don't lie to yourself—that is all of us!) might be tempted to believe that we are begging or groveling or in some way appearing weak. Get over it and ask for what you want. You will not die from asking for support, and polite but assertive requests show strength, not weakness.

As a part of your planning, think about the questions you might want to ask. A networking meeting or telephone conversation does not have to be limited to asking your contact about positions in his or her organization. You might also ask about:

- Any positions he or she may have heard about in other organizations

- Other individuals that he or she would suggest you contact

- Any introductions that he or she would be willing to provide to other influential individuals

- Any other advice or ideas that he or she may have for you in your pursuit

## Keep Working Your List

A networking list should be an organic tool. It can grow as new contacts are added and shrink as some turn out to be less productive. A word of caution: Be careful about divorcing your contacts—that's deleting names of people on your list who upset you by not calling back or who seem not to care. Sometimes others are genuinely too busy to help at the time, but on a different day and in different circumstances, these same people could have a lot of valuable support for you. Don't give up on others because they are fallible human beings. You are too.

Even if you are having a conflict with someone, a burned bridge will never support you in the future. The world is a small place and people do come back around in our lives. We can forget and they can forget. You never know, so swallow your ego and keep every potential relationship at least neutral. It never pays to burn one.

Once you have created your list, begin to work it. A lot of job seekers occasionally lose energy and their psychological persistence and stop calling. That's okay for a short time, as the job of finding a path forward can be tiring and at times even depressing.

I have seen individuals contact everyone on their list and then sit and wait. There is a common delusion that once someone says, "Oh definitely, I will keep my eyes open for you!" that they are on a constant environmental scan, a search mission to help. In a world of high unemployment, influential people might hear from someone else looking for work almost every day. It might seem cruel, but others forget about us, and nobody thinks about our wishes and desires as much as we do.

The implication is that we have to work our list. Each contact should be put on a schedule for follow-up based on each person's level of activity in support of our cause. If someone plans to make a critical call on our behalf, the follow-up might be in twenty-four hours or the next week. If a person is an important ally or mentor, maybe every thirty days is the right cadence. Others might be scheduled on a quarterly basis or every six months. The message here is regular contact with those on our list. Don't assume they are thinking about you. Help them to remember.

Besides one-to-one networking, many job searchers find benefit in networking groups. Attending a support group meeting to share and learn best practices can be useful, and sometimes it is consoling to realize you are not alone. Good outplacement firms often sponsor these groups, and there are other options based on industry and location.

One powerful way to use networking is to first select the organizations that you would really like to work for. Create a criteria filter that makes them great organizations for you. For example, besides being rated by publications like *Fortune* magazine as one of the best places to work, you might admire certain organizations for their culture, their leadership, their customer values, or maybe because of their market leadership.

Once you have selected one or more organizations that make your favorites list, ask everyone in your network if they have any connections there or would be willing to make any introductions for you. It is always amazing how resourceful others can be in helping you find what you want.

One of the magic facets of good networking is how often a contact remarks, "You know, it is great that you called, and I was just thinking about calling you. I just heard about an opportunity that might fit your talents last week!" Maybe the contact was going to call, or maybe she forgot about your search. You will never know. But the remarkable synchronicity is that staying in touch with others so often produces unexpected benefits. Staying in touch with people makes a difference.

One of the practical lessons is that we should be good networkers all of the time, even when we don't need something back in return. We all know this, and we all forget or get too busy. One of the benefits of online social networking can be to stay in touch in a relatively unobtrusive way, but in keeping the relationship fresh and current.

Sometimes it takes a crisis in our lives to remind us of what we already know. People who have been good at maintaining their networks before they are starting over can hit the ground running.

## The Role of Ego

A few more reflections on the role of ego and networking. These points have already been made in one way or another, but pride and arrogance can get in the way of a successful search. If others believe that you are making a genuine plea for support, they can do incredible things to help. On the other hand, if you are acting prideful or being a rugged individualist, others might just let you rise or fall on your own. Don't pretend that everything is just fine when it is not. If you need help, don't be afraid to ask for it.

For those who have not been in a professional sales role, the fear of rejection coupled with fear of the unknown can cause people to act in self-destructive ways. If people define themselves as their jobs, and interpret their worth as a function of their past status, it becomes more difficult to ask for support.

None of us wants to lose face, so it is important to look inside ourselves for our dignity, not in any outside trappings or images. Otherwise good networking can feel like begging, and if we believe we are begging, we will not be at our best at a time when we need to.

When our egos control us, networking e-mails and telephone calls that go unanswered can lead to negative self-talk. *I can't believe that jerk doesn't have the decency to just call me back. After all I have done.* Or maybe we begin to think, *To heck with him! I don't need his help, I'll do this on my own.* Or maybe we even begin to think, *I don't have any value left to add—they were right.* Of course it is pretty embarrassing when our contact comes back from a long vacation and calls us on Monday morning.

Salespeople deal with this kind of rejection all of the time and sometimes even get used to it. If someone has not experienced professional rejection or maybe worse yet if he has been in an organization that worships technical expertise, this kind of rejection can be very difficult to swallow. The preference for an expert is to drop hints that he is available and then sit back and wait for a call, to let someone else find him. Whenever you feel rejection in a serious life search, it's important to let it go and to move on.

In 2009, Tiger Woods failed to make the cut at the British Open at Turnberry in Ayrshire, Scotland. It was only the second time in

Tiger's thirteen-year professional career that he had missed a cut at a major tournament. It was the first time he had been excluded from the final rounds at any tournament in more than three years. The only other time Tiger had missed the cut at a major tournament was right after his father, Earle, had passed away.

In the next two weeks, he came back and won the Buick Open and the Bridgestone Invitational, consecutively.

When asked how he recovered from his devastating loss in Scotland to win the Buick Open, Tiger simply mentioned that, as a professional golfer, you can't carry losses forward. You have to let them go and move on to the next tournament.

The same is true for anyone starting over in their careers. If we let any event or circumstance drain energy away from the task at hand, we won't be as effective. We won't do our best. If someone loses a job, has a contact who doesn't call back, fails in an interview, or even works for a full year on an opportunity that doesn't pan out, she needs to leave it behind. Let it go and move on. This is why managing our egos in the journey of starting over is so critical.

Any self-talk, thoughts, or emotions that detract from our energy hold us back. Whether they are true or not, any roadblocks or obstacles that we throw in front of ourselves will slow us down, and maybe even stop us in our tracks. Self-talk, thoughts, and emotions that build positive energy help us.

In his insightful book, *The Power of Intention*, Wayne Dyer[32] describes interfering ego in six elements:

1. I am what I have—I measure my worth on the value of my material belongings.
2. I am what I do—I am my achievements.
3. I am my reputation—I am what everybody else thinks of me.
4. I am separate from everybody else.

5. I am separate from the things that are missing in my life (as opposed to I am already connected to everything I believe is missing).
6. Who I am is separate from God.

When our egos get strong, when any of these six elements of ego are working in our lives, we don't come across with the best we have to offer. When we stop trying to be the best in the world, and become our best for the world, our true strengths emerge. And the people who will consider you for a role in their organizations, as well as the network of people who will help you, will see you for who you are.

The worst part of a dysfunctional ego might be the emotional pain people encounter on their search. Letting go of our egos, or at least keeping them at bay, makes the journey much more enjoyable. After a time of loss it is natural to be insecure about the future and to lose some self-confidence. Our egos love that opening.

Maybe ego is how we protect ourselves during difficult times. The paradox is that letting go of our egos allows our inner strengths, the true people that we really are, to shine through.

Getting to acceptance of our current state and then making the best of it, doing what we can control, is the fastest way to get started on the next growth curve. Getting rid of ego helps to reduce the cycle time in getting to acceptance.

## Go for It

One of the most practical pieces of advice that I would offer to anyone starting over is to take action. Don't simply sit to reflect and make notes of creative ideas. Create a marketing plan for yourself if you want, but don't stop there. Define your value proposition and your personal brand identity, but then go communicate them to everyone.

Call someone, schedule an interview, complete an application for employment, or write a letter to a prospective employer. Find a search specialist to help you, and don't be afraid to contact several. If those actions don't work out, learn from them, and do something else.

One of the worst parts of a new career search is waiting. So take a lot of actions and keep moving forward. Create a path forward plan, but then execute it. The worst that can happen is the plan won't work. If you come to believe in playing to win, you can never fail, you can only do your best working toward your goals. In the end, it will work out for you.

I like to challenge people who are searching to believe with all of their hearts that their search will work out. When someone knows that their search will work out, the ride to the next curve becomes much more enjoyable. When you get to the other side you will see. You will say, "This really worked out. I wish I had reflected more and enjoyed the journey!"

Keep moving ahead and you will see.

"Everything works out in the end. If it hasn't worked out, it's not the end."

—Unknown

# 11

## Finding the Right Support

> "We are not sure who first discovered water,
> but we are pretty sure it wasn't a fish."
>
> —Marshall McLuhan

### A Fish out of Water

From time to time, life reminds us that we need one another. During times of major life transition such as the loss of a loved one, a health crisis, or a separation, one life chapter ends and another begins. Starting over in our lives is one of those times. We need help.

It's possible that challenging events just happen, not by any grand design, but by virtue of a random universe, where "stuff happens." But I don't think so. Too many bigger patterns emerge through our lives not to believe in a bigger scheme at hand. Either way—we need support in challenging times.

Maybe life introduces those occasions to teach us a universal lesson: we are here on earth to collaborate, to help each other along step-by-step to a better life.

Like Marshall McLuhan's fish, we are not always conscious of the principles in action, until the *water* is gone. When the water is always present—that is, when life has been stable and abundant for a time—we take stability and prosperity for granted. They are always there, they have always been there. When the water is taken away, when we experience a disruption in life's flow, we remember once again. We need a hand from others to get through.

In light of the grander scheme of things, what is the purpose of relationships? For one thing, the people around us serve as mirrors, to reflect back to us who we are—our strengths, our weaknesses, our comfort zones, our foibles, and our quirky ways of making sense of it all.

Each person we meet, by virtue of his or her own persona, provides feedback to us. If we pay attention, they help us to learn about our own nature. If we choose to listen, others can help us learn and grow and to better understand the lessons we are here to learn.

When someone decides to commit to the game of growth and learning in life, relationships become essential.

Another way to think about the purpose of relationships is that others have messages for us to help us navigate through life, and, in turn, we have messages for them. This is the inherent value in earth's diversity. We could never see as much on our own.

What can we learn from one another along the path? For one, life is too complex to navigate alone. No matter how smart, nobody can see it all. The lessons are already there; we just need each other to see and learn them.

Searching for a next career step is too complex and difficult to do alone. Maybe this complexity is why we witness the amazing power of networking during a job search. When we let everyone in the world know that we are looking, the strength of relationships becomes obvious.

We need the personal and emotional support that gives us the strength—the fuel—to get through this difficult time.

## Support, Not Sympathy

Good support is not the same as good sympathy. We don't need someone to slink down into a victim mindset with us when things get tough. In fact, good support often means *tough love*, offered by someone who won't accept our excuses when things get difficult.

We don't need someone who simply goes along with us. Consider the following two lists: one of reasons for not finding a new job and one of reasons for finding one:

<table>
<tr><td>

<u>Reasons for Not Finding a Job</u>

</td><td>

<u>Reasons for Finding a Job</u>

</td></tr>
<tr><td>

- Hundreds of people apply for every job out there.

- Everyone sees the same jobs online, so what chance do I have?

- With jobs so tight, people get hired for political reasons.

- Prospective employers have software that sorts through resumes looking for key words that I don't even know.

- I'll never find another job in this economy.

- This is too hard!

- This is more than I can handle.

</td><td>

- I bring enough value to my search to stand out. I have a unique brand identity.

- I will hear about unique opportunities through timely networking.

- I will get hired because of my relationships and my ability to quickly form relationships.

- I will use active language in my resume that describes my unique talents, and the right job will pick me.

- My search might take longer in this economy, but eventually I will find a job. I just need one job, and it is waiting out there for me.

- This is hard and any real accomplishments are hard.

- I can find ways to increase my capacity to handle more.

</td></tr>
</table>

Realistically, which of these two lists is true? Actually, they are both true. They are equally accurate descriptions of a job search during difficult times.

Which way of thinking will help someone find a job? Maybe neither. But my money is on the reasons *why*, not the reasons *why not*. If it is true that with psychological persistence someone will eventually find a job, the journey is much more pleasant on the right-hand side. It is a choice.

In difficult times, some people will always succeed. Except for a total annihilation of the earth, some human beings will survive the worst of conditions. People who thrive are more likely to believe that they can succeed and that it is possible. They have self-efficacy.

They have an internal focus of control, meaning they believe they are in control of their destinies, not an external focus of control, in which they believe control lies outside of them.

When it comes to real support from others, we need people who will not let us believe in the left-hand column or sidle up to us in pity. We need constructive support from people who drag us over to the right-hand column, who remind us about our strengths when we whine or get stuck in the past. For any difficult challenge there is a long list of reasons why and a long list why not, and we get to the end of the race much faster believing *why*.

When starting over, we need to get cynics and doubters out of our lives.

It is impossible to get everyone to support us, much like it is impossible to get everyone to like us. What would the people who would judge and disparage us say?

The only answer to this question has to be, "It doesn't really matter!"

We are tempted during hard times to be discouraged and to imagine what our naysayers would say, but we have to support ourselves too and put it out of our minds. We need to be our own best friend during tough times.

Any self-talk or talk from others that detracts from our commitment to succeed in our mission has to go. Most likely, we will never know what our critics say because they probably won't say it to our faces. But it doesn't matter. There is no value for judgment and criticism in a difficult transition. We need to ignore it and surround ourselves with people who genuinely care for us and support us.

If we can answer the question, "What are my critics saying about me?" that's a danger sign, because it means that we are likely rehearsing the answer. The list of things our critics would say is a self-compiled list that we make up, and the time and energy spent in creating it is wasted.

Early scientific studies to determine if a high-fiber diet reduces "bad" cholesterol (LDL) were inconclusive. Subsequent research has demonstrated a positive, causal effect. But at the time, some observers noticed that eating foods that are high in fiber and low in saturated fats simply replaced alternative foods that were high in saturated fats and created an elevation in cholesterol. Scientists couldn't prove at the time that fiber reduced cholesterol, but high-fiber foods replaced other foods that did cause it.

Thinking positive thoughts about yourself and your abilities is similar. It's important to surround ourselves with people who reinforce those positive self-images, and stay away from well-meaning friends who are cynics, whiners, and victims.

## An Emotional Choice

Mike Redick found himself in a pickle. Like so many others in the same boat, he had been outplaced from his company. Suddenly Mike found himself out of work for the first time in his life. Ever since he could remember, he had always been busy with school and work, with more to do than twenty-four hours allowed. Life surprises many adults who imagine a more even script, and now he had to rethink everything.

Mike is an ambitious and driven professional who got right to work on his search, but even for the best of us, the job of looking for a job is hard. In his own optimistic way, Mike noticed the silver linings in the process. Crisis always creates opportunities for our core values to emerge and for the good in us to come out. He found a great deal of meaning in talking about the experience of being let go. He found compassion from the people who listened. Still, talking about his job loss was difficult, embarrassing, and awkward.

*After all I had done, didn't they think that I was worth holding on to?*

It was difficult for Mike to tell other people that he was unemployed. Ironically, a good networker quickly learns that is exactly what is needed. Other people didn't see Mike's job loss as a failure at all. It happens every day. We are not the roles we play in our lives, and our success as human beings is not about our triumphs or our disappointments on the job. We are not our work.

So being open about job loss is a first, simple step. Of course simple doesn't equate to easy.

Mike found a telephone support group that he called into every Monday morning for thirty minutes. The teleconference was a way to start the week that helped him get on course and to focus on his search. He also found a support group at the First Presbyterian Church called the Tuesday Night Group. It was not about crying on shoulders but just getting common sense advice from others with similar issues. The group was about having someone to talk to.

Mike discovered that it was important to schedule interviews and to create opportunities for more interviews, even those that didn't seem like a perfect fit. It was good for him to get out to interact with others and especially to be reminded of the value that he was bringing to the marketplace. He had skills and he had successes to talk about—Mike was good at what he did. He also learned the fine art of networking, of reaching out to everyone he knew, to spread the word and to ask for support.

Unless someone has professional experience in sales, many are not ready to sell themselves. Many view selling as an activity way out of their comfort zones. Selling yourself is the whole point, though. That is the primary job at hand.

Back in the 1990s, when there were not enough good people to take all of the jobs in a booming economy, many people waited for the offers to come in and for the calls that came from the search specialists. The '90s were a time that built egos and arrogance and planted the seeds for false expectations when those same people had to look for a job. The offers were not there, and the disillusionment followed.

Finding constructive job search activities for ten hours a day is difficult. So Mike also took some time to do some of the real-life things that he had put off in the past. He took time to volunteer, to give back, and personally discovered the wisdom in Gandhi's message to "find yourself by losing yourself in the service of others." He helped to raise funds for community projects and got more involved in his local school board.

These seemingly extracurricular activities actually led to the discovery of some job openings and good networking. The change of pace and pleasure from getting out of the home office was one of the best aspects, though. Even when time in a search seems critical, personal balance in mind, body, and spirit allows you to be at your best when the interviews do come.

Three aspects of the experience turned out to be Mike's biggest challenges.

1. Making his search a full-time job was a large burden for Mike to carry. Despite a serious effort, anyone who is used to going to an office struggles with working out of his or her home, on the kitchen table or in a spare bedroom. It feels unnatural, and many find themselves drifting about to break the tedium and discomfort.

2. After a sudden departure from his company (aren't they all?), Mike struggled to find clarity in his new identity, which was really about letting go of a past identity and the status that is embedded in a title. *I used to be a director at my company. What do I tell my peers, my acquaintances, my neighbors, and even my friends? All of a sudden I was on the street. Who am I now?*

3. Mike reflected on his denial during the evolution of his job loss: *I should have known better and seen the downsizing coming. I knew in my heart what was going to happen, and I just put my head down and worked harder. I should have been out looking for a new job sooner, because it is a lot easier to look for a job when you already have one. I felt stupid and naïve to not face reality and do something sooner.*

Happily, despite these challenges, the story ended well for Mike as he found a good job that paid well with potential for even more than he was making in the past. His challenges are universal in the job search process, and his reaction at the end was too: *This is a better life than I had in the past. You know, I should have left my old job a long time ago!*

I suppose it doesn't end well for many, like the people who find jobs that pay less, or those who lose appreciable personal wealth or go into debt while searching for something new. Some might find jobs where they don't really fit or don't have a chance to use their full talents.

But the people whom I have coached consistently live a story that ends with Mike's revelation: *I should have done this a long time ago. You know, there really is life after (fill in the blank)!*

Life's stories can end well when we are willing to work hard for what we want. Searching for that next phase in life is really about getting through the transition. Success requires having faith, even though the end result is not at all what we had planned when we started the change.

Success also means building emotional strength, the capacity to raise your threshold for the pain and frustration inherent in the journey. Getting to the destination is a matter of doing the right things and yet, at the same time, accepting the new reality by managing the emotional side of the change. Effective change management is an emotional skill as much as an intellectual skill. A key to starting over is EQ, emotional quotient, as much as IQ.

## We Need Support

Successful employers want individualists as well as collaborators. High performers accept personal accountability for the results they create and don't look toward others. We need to be able to stand on our own, to leave whatever nest keeps us dependent, so we can walk our own paths.

But at the same time, we need each other too. As O. Hobart Mowrer said, "You alone can do it, but you cannot do it alone."

We hesitate to give others support when focused on our own agendas, and we certainly avoid asking for support. None of us would be successful in our lives without the support of others. And yet we seem hesitant to ask for it when we need it the most.

Support can come from any number of people around us, but our network of resources can be one of the best places to look.

The kind of support we often give to each other reinforces our victim mindsets: *Nobody is hiring right now, that's for sure!* or *I'd like to see Steve Jobs come run some of these companies. Then we'd see some new jobs!*

There is a cynical brand of humor made famous by Dilbert cartoons that is alive and well in America. For any of us who have witnessed the foibles of corporate America, it seems impossible not to laugh. Then almost unconsciously, it is easy to strengthen each other's pessimism about the future.

People who are starting over need support for taking personal responsibility, not support for giving up. We need people in our lives who encourage us to create good habits in mind, body, and spirit, and to help us change the game. Getting the right support also requires letting go of whatever gets in the way of asking, whether it is our egos, our pride, or our rugged individualism.

The challenge is to decide who can provide that kind of support for you, then to be willing to ask and be willing to give too. A key is to make a conscious decision about what support you will need and then to engineer it to make sure it happens.

## Support Tools and Techniques

Here are ideas and tools adapted from *Finding Personal Balance*[33] that you might use to find support from others as you work through life transition:

1. **Find a support buddy:** Find someone who is willing to be your guardian angel—who will look out for you and act as your conscience. A real support buddy cares about you and is someone who is truly committed to your success in finding the next step in your career. He or she is willing to hold the mirror up to you, to use tough love if needed to keep you on track. A good support buddy is someone with whom you can talk openly and who will in turn talk openly with you, especially when you need it.

2. **Create a support group:** Maybe a small group of friends would work for you—a small support group to keep you focused on your search. Maybe you would be more comfortable in joining a professional support group. Weight Watchers has used this principle very successfully, as have many twelve-step groups fighting their addictions. The point is to be accountable to others, which is a strong motivator in any new venture.

3.  **Be honest about your weaknesses:** Predict ahead of time when you will lose focus or energy and structure your environment to avoid loss of momentum. If you struggle to get up in the morning, schedule an early time with a personal trainer and promise not to skip your workout. (*Hurt me, Helga!*) Ask your significant other or best friend to ask for progress updates. Make a public commitment to your friends and family and ask for their feedback.

4.  **Keep a journal:** Write things down, including your goals, your commitments, your positive affirmations, and your progress.

5.  **Publicly post commitments:** Write out your life vision and your goals on a note card and post it above your desk or on your refrigerator, so you keep a compelling vision in front of you. Think of Tino Wallenda aiming for that other platform. Maybe you could make your compelling vision your screen saver.

6.  **Teach others:** Sharing your knowledge with others reinforces your own commitment. Teaching others is a great reminder of the things that you already know you need to do.

7.  **Get on your knees:** Give up control to a higher power and then listen for the guidance that will come your way.

"Our dilemma is that we hate change and love it at the same time; what we really want is for things to remain the same but get better."

—Sydney J. Harris

# 12

## Take Care of Yourself

"Don't let go of the vine."

—Johnny Weissmuller (Hollywood's Tarzan, 1932–1948)

### Take Time

On top of the pressure to redefine your life mission, the financial aspects of starting a life over can lead to an acute sense of urgency. People find ways to survive by borrowing money, using their savings, accepting support from family and friends, selling belongings, or whatever it takes. Savers are rewarded for their conservative habits. Those who have saved less wish they had saved more. No matter how diligent you have been in the past, however, you may feel pressure to reach a rapid resolution.

There is a cumulative pressure that can build as a search progresses. Even retirees who are not looking for work but simply exploring new lives go through a difficult transition period. Everyone wonders, *Will I ever find what I am looking for? Will my resources last?*

When starting over, taking care of yourself—of mind, body, and spirit—becomes all the more critical. Even in a difficult routine, there is comfort in the routine itself. During a job and a life search people need an increased capacity to manage stress.

Observed from the outside, someone might appear to be doing very little. And yet life can feel like a pressure cooker. There is no choice but to get through it—to fight the battle and to win.

Taking time off is an ironic concept for someone who doesn't have a full-time job. *Time off from what?* A diligent search is a full-time endeavor, though. It's important to take some time for yourself despite the apparent urgency to survive and to find a next job.

The goal is to show up for that next interview refreshed and at your best. That doesn't mean that job seekers are entitled to the four weeks of vacation they got on the last job, but it's important to incorporate healthy and healing approaches to life every day.

## Threshold

Another of Bill Harris's *nine principles for conscious living* is the notion of "threshold".[34] The idea is that each person has a threshold for handling what's coming at him or her in life. When stress surpasses a person's threshold, the pressure gets too high, and people experience negative reactions.

Individuals have low thresholds, or a low tolerance for stressful life events, when they have a history of traumatic experiences that have caused negative emotional responses. People who are exposed to a high-stress environment for a prolonged period of time also have lower thresholds. Evidence of a low personal threshold becomes apparent in regularly occurring reactions like high frustration, anger, fear, guilt, or anxiety. Signs of being over one's threshold can range from a general nervousness or free-floating anxiety to post-traumatic stress syndrome (PTSS).

Life events such as child abuse leave victims struggling to cope. Such events lower that individual's threshold for the future. Children don't have the capacity to deal with trauma. If a home doesn't feel safe, for example, when a parent is a drug abuser or an alcoholic, the effects can last a lifetime.

Experiences in war can reduce personal threshold. Veterans from every war, including Iraq and Afghanistan, say that the reality of war is nothing like the movies. War is the harshest of realities where nearly every moment is literally focused on survival. The constant tension can be unbearable as evidenced by the frequency of post-traumatic stress syndrome, an outcome referred to in earlier wars as "shell shock."

Even poor work processes over a period of time can reduce personal threshold. Frustration from work can cause lingering effects including a reduced emotional tolerance for the challenges life brings. People develop an expectation of negative events and develop an external focus of control. The outcome can be a generalized loss of energy or *burnout*.

Another indicator of high stress can be observed when people go over their thresholds for minor things, such as over-reacting to poor service in a restaurant or in response to other drivers on the highway. However, the solution is not always reducing the negative inputs from life.

We don't always have a choice in what life hands us. We rarely drive alone on the roads. We need to raise our thresholds and increase our abilities to cope with any future events, no matter what happens.

In one sense, people are open systems, with inputs and outputs, and when the inputs get to be too much, we go over our thresholds.

There are three common responses to stress that put us over our thresholds:

1. **We attempt to block the input**: If an upstream dam begins to leak and the river gets too high, we try to plug the leak, to slow the input. People do this with stressful life events by avoiding, escaping, or leaving a situation such as a job or a relationship. We might even get depressed. Depression is a natural way to heal the body and the mind by stopping

the flow of life for a time, and it is a healthy response when we are in true grief. However, none of these responses is a healthy way to cope with life on an ongoing basis.

2. **We attempt to increase the output, to release the energy**: A second response when the river gets high is to open our own dam to get rid of the excess water. In the emotional sense, we try to release the excess stress. People do this in all kinds of ways, some socially acceptable and some not. For example, some like to exercise, talk to someone in their support network, meditate or pray, which are all healthy.

Others exercise excessively, overeat, under-eat or "shop till they drop." Some become obsessed with online navigation, texting, social networking, e-mail, video games, or computer games. In July 2009 ReSTART, the first residential treatment center for Internet addiction opened its doors in Fall City, Washington, offering a forty-five day program to help people break online addiction.

Some people drive fast and others talk incessantly while at the same time becoming a challenge to be around, adding even more stress to their friends and coworkers. Certain individuals complain about everything and nag or criticize everyone within earshot. Humans use an unlimited number of compulsive behaviors in an attempt to find release, just to feel good again. We are very creative in finding ways to let go of excess energy and stress.

3. **We anesthetize ourselves**: We medicate ourselves with alcohol, drugs (legalized and not), and comfort food. It is much like receiving nitrous oxide and oxygen at the dentist. The pain is still there, but at least temporarily, we don't seem to care anymore.

## Become More Buoyant

What becomes obvious is that, at best, when our stress goes beyond our threshold, the best option is to find a healthy means of release. In some ways we might be able to block stressful events, but in real life that is a temporary option.

We rely on vacations and other forms of escape when we should be finding daily solutions, not annual getaways.

When we surpass our thresholds, putting life's events on pause, finding unhealthy release, and medicating ourselves are not wholesome choices. When the river gets high, the best alternative is to become more buoyant, to raise our thresholds, so that challenging life events don't create stress in the first place. This approach means preparing ourselves for whatever happens—increasing the emotional capacity to deal with any input or life event.

It really comes back to letting whatever happens be okay, to accept what life brings instead of denying or resisting.

Someone who is starting over in his career may not have a short-term choice of getting another job. His income may be stopped and his life mission placed on hold. There is simply no immediate solution, especially in difficult times, when good jobs are scarce or someone is looking for a senior-level role, where opportunities are scarce. There is no switch to flip to just make life better.

Even if we don't have a choice in what life brings, we *always* have a choice in how we respond to life—how we think, feel, and act. Increasing

> The Serenity Prayer
>
> God grant me the serenity
> to accept the things
> I cannot change,
> the courage to change the
> things I can,
> and the wisdom to know
> the difference.
>
> - Reinhold Niebuhr

emotional capacity is a matter of conscious change and of a commitment to personal growth.

As in the Serenity Prayer, peace of mind comes through finding acceptance, courage, and wisdom, no matter what happens. This is the emotional obligation of anyone starting over, to prepare for whatever happens. No matter what. What if this is as good as it gets?

## Find Personal Balance

So finding your personal balance, taking care of yourself during difficult transition, is essential to coming back out to the world in the best possible way. To maintain health during difficult times, you need to pay attention to every facet of the whole person:

1. **Mind:** How do you think about the world around you, as evidenced by your *self-talk*? How do you harness perhaps the strongest resource in existence, the human mind? Are you choosing the mindsets that will help you achieve the outcomes you want? You have the final freedom—to choose how you think and feel, no matter what happens. But you are the only one who can make that choice.

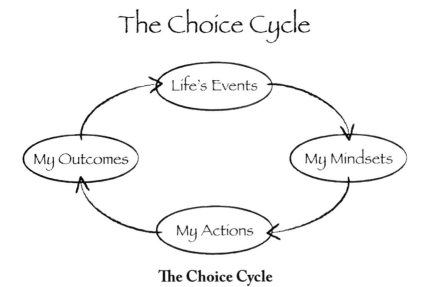

**The Choice Cycle**

2. **Body:** How will you take care of your physical health, through diet, exercise, and sleep, to strengthen the connection between your physiological foundation and your emotional health?

3. **Spirit:** How will you employ some form of meditative practice or prayer to regularly *still the waters*—to practice reaching a deep sense of calm in your life? How will you live in the moment and let go of any emotional baggage from the past as well as fear of the future? How will you come to assume that life will work out? How will you become a part of something bigger than yourself?

4. **Simplicity:** How will you define your priorities and reduce the complexity in your life so your mission to move forward becomes paramount? How will you create a physical environment and structure in your life that supports the health of your mind, body, and spirit?

5. **Support:** How can you create the right support system—one that will help you be the person you really want to be?

## We Already Have It

In so many ways starting over is a mental and an emotional game. Beginning again in our life is something that we all try very hard to avoid while we attempt to cling to some imagined security. Life reminds us frequently that security in our human experience is an illusion.

The wonderful part of beginning a new life cycle is that, while the time can be filled with challenge, in retrospect, it is also a phase of great personal growth and learning. Starting over can be a time to anneal our inner strength.

Perhaps the greatest lesson that life can teach us by stripping away all we have for a time—our jobs, incomes, status, and egos—is to teach us that those things have never really been the true source of our happiness anyway.

When we are left alone with ourselves, we have the opportunity to look inside and see that what we are looking for was right there all of the time. We have everything we need inside us to find peace right now.

"Let me not pray to be sheltered from dangers
but to be fearless in facing them.
Let me not beg for the stilling of my pain,
but for the heart to conquer it.
Let me not look for allies in life's battlefield
but to my own strength.
Let me not crave in anxious fear to be saved but
hope for the patience to win my freedom.
Grant me that I may not be a coward, feeling
your mercy in my success alone;
But let me find the grasp of your hand in my failure."

—Rabindranath Tagore

# Some Reading for Life Transition

Are you looking for other books to read during a life transition? Here are some of the books that have helped on my own personal journey. Perhaps there is something here for you—a book with a message for you—a lesson that you are waiting to receive.

Here are my favorites:

Will Ellis, *Finding Personal Balance: A Path to Inner Peace in a Life of Doing More* (iUniverse, Inc., 2008).

M. Scott Peck, M.D., *The Road Less Traveled: A New Psychology of Love, Traditional Values, and Spiritual Growth* (New York, NY: A Touchstone Book published by Simon & Schuster, 1978).

M. Scott Peck, M.D., *The Different Drum: Community Making and Peace* (New York, NY: A Touchstone Book, published by Simon & Schuster, Inc., 1987).

Viktor E. Frankl, *Man's Search for Meaning* (Boston: Beacon Press, 2000), 26.

Trisha Meili, *I Am the Central Park Jogger: A Story of Hope and Possibility* (New York: Scribner, 2004).

Marianne Williamson, *A Return To Love: Reflections on the Principles of "A Course in Miracles"* (New York, NY: HarperCollins Publishers, Inc., 1992).

Brennan Manning, *Ruthless Trust: The Ragamuffin's Path to God* (New York, NY: HarperCollins Publishers, Inc., 2000).

Oriah Mountain Dreamer, *The Dance: Moving to the Rhythms of Your True Self* (New York, NY: HarperCollins Publishers, Inc., 2001).

Greg Mortenson and David Oliver Relin, *Three Cups of Tea: One Man's Mission to Promote Peace … One School at a Time* (Penguin Books, 2006).

William P. Young, *The Shack* (Windblown Media, 2007).

Deepak Chopra, *The Seven Spiritual Laws of Success: A Practical Guide to the Fulfillment of Your Dreams* (San Rafael, CA: Amber-Allen Publishing, 1994).

Shunryu Suzuki, *Zen Mind, Beginner's Mind: Informal talks on Zen Meditation and Practice* (New York, NY: Weatherhill, Inc., 1995).

Pema Chödrön, *When Things Fall Apart: Heart Advice for Difficult Times* (Boston, MA: Shambala Publications, Inc., 1997).

Pema Chödrön, *Start Where You Are: A Guide to Compassionate Living* (Boston, MA: Shambala Publications, Inc., 2001).

Wayne W. Dyer, *There's A Spiritual Solution to Every Problem* (New York, NY: HarperCollins Publishers, Inc., 2001).

Wayne W. Dyer, *Getting In The Gap: Making Conscious Contact with God Through Meditation* (Carlsbad, CA: Hay House Inc., 2003).

Wayne W. Dyer, *Change Your Thoughts—Change Your Life: Living the Wisdom of the Tao* (Carlsbad, CA: Hay House Inc., 2007).

Bill Harris, *Thresholds of the Mind: Your Personal Roadmap to Success, Happiness, and Contentment* (Beaverton, OR: Centerpointe Press, Centerpointe Research Institute, 2007).

*The Bible*

Add your own books to this list and pass it along to someone you care about.

# Notes

1   Mary Chapin Carpenter, "10,000 miles," Sony Music, 1989.

2   Emily Kaiser, Nick Carey, and Tim Gaynor, "The Price of U.S. Recession is Paid in Jobs," *Yahoo! News*, August 3, 2009.

3   Eugene O'Kelly with Andrew Postman, *Chasing Daylight: How My Forthcoming Death Transformed My Life* (McGraw-Hill, 2006).

4   Brennan Manning, *Ruthless Trust: The Ragamuffin's Path to God* (HarperSanFrancisco, Harper Collins, 2000), 5.

5   Bill Harris, *Thresholds of the Mind: Your Personal Roadmap to Success, Happiness and Contentment* (Beaverton, Oregon: Centerpointe Press, 2007), 127–50.

6   O'Kelly, ibid.

7   Parker J. Palmer, "Seasons: A Center for Renewal," The Fetzer Institute, Kalamazoo, Michigan.

8   Paul J. Steinhardt and Neil Turok, *Endless Universe: Beyond the Big Bang* (Doubleday Publishing, 2007).

9   Peter B. Vaill, *Learning as a Way of Being: Strategies for Survival in a World of Permanent White Water* (Jossey-Bass Inc., 1996).

10  George T. Ainsworth-Land, *Grow or Die: The Unifying Principle of Transformation* (John Wiley & Sons Inc., 1986).

11  Seth Godin, *The Dip: The Little Book that Teaches You When to Quit (And When to Stick)* (Penguin Books Ltd., 2007).

12  Economic News Release, "Number of Jobs Held, Labor Market Activity, and Earnings Growth among the Youngest Baby Boomers: Results from a Longitudinal Survey Summary" (United States Department of Labor, Bureau of Labor Statistics, June 27, 2008).

13  John C. Maxwell, *Failing Forward: Turning Mistakes into Stepping Stones for Success* (Thomas Nelson, Inc., 2000).

14  Godin, ibid., 33–4.

15  Scott Shane, *The Illusions of Entrepreneurship: The Costly Myths that Entrepreneurs, Investors, and Policy Makers Live By* (Yale University Press, 2008).

16  Jim Collins, *Good to Great: Why Some Companies Make the Leap and Others Don't* (HarperCollins Publishers, Inc., 2001).

17  Jim Collins, *How the Mighty Fall and Why Some Companies Never Give In* (HarperCollins Publishers, Inc., 2009).

18  Tom Krishner and Dan Strumpf, "GM CEO Wagoner Forced Out as Part of Government Plan, *Yahoo News*, March 30, 2009.

19  Sinclair Stewart, "Wagoner's Legacy: A Culture of Compromise" *CTVglobalmedia Publishing, Inc.*, March 31, 2009.

20  *Wang Laboratories* (Wikipedia, http://en.wikipedia.org/wiki/Wang_Laboratories)

21  *The Unofficial Wang VS Information Center*, http://www.tjunker.com/pagabtwg.html.

22 IBM Archives, http://www-03.ibm.com/ibm/history/exhibits/.

23 Godin, ibid.

24 Elisabeth Kübler-Ross, *On Death and Dying* (Scribner, 1969).

25 Will Ellis, *Finding Personal Balance: A Path to Inner Peace in a Life of Doing More* (iUniverse, Inc., 2008).

26 Warren Bennis and Burt Nanus, *Leaders: The Strategies for Taking Charge* (Harper Collins, 2003).

27 Rhonda Byrne, *The Secret* (Atria Books, 2006).

28 *The Secret* (Prime Time Productions, 2006, http://www.thesecret.tv/).

29 G. Jeffrey MacDonald, "Does Maya Calendar Predict 2012 Apocalypse?" *USAToday.com*, March 27, 2007, http://www.usatoday.com/tech/science/2007-03-27-maya-2012_n.htm.

30 Larry Wilson and Hersch Wilson, *Play to Win: Choosing Growth over Fear in Work and Life* (Bard Press, Inc., 1998)

31 John Wooden and Steve Jamison, *Wooden on Leadership* (McGraw-Hill, 2005), 8–9.

32 Wayne W. Dyer, *The Power of Intention: Learning to Co-create Your World Your Way* (Hay House, Inc., 2004).

33 Ellis, ibid.

34 Harris, ibid, 130.

CPSIA information can be obtained
at www.ICGtesting.com
Printed in the USA
LVOW10*0629011116

511058LV00004B/10/P

9 781440 190315